KEYS TO BEING SOCIAL

Being Real in a Virtual World

Bridget Willard

BridgetWillard.com

ISBN-13: 9798695010756

Cover design by: Rhonda Negard
Library of Congress Control Number: 2018675309
Printed in the United States of America

To You

CONTENTS

INTRODUCTION

To do well with social media, you need the right set of keys. The right keys let us open our cars, offices, homes, mailboxes, and garages. Keys are uniquely shaped to their corresponding lock or entry system. Each key gives us the ability to utilize a specific tool we own to manage our responsibilities and interests.

Social media is a simple tool we can use to manage our responsibilities and interests *if* we own the right set of keys. And like so many other power tools, many people are intimidated by the opportunity to pick up this tool and utilize it. Just like turning on a chainsaw can be intimidating. Still, once you turn it on, you realize it's not so hard to turn it on and off, but you also know you have no idea how to safely chop down a big tree in the middle of a forest. You would need specific training on the how-and-why of chainsaw usage.

Using social media isn't so different. The technology itself can be intimidating, but the technology is easy to teach. It's the philosophy, the how-and-why social media strategies that will make all of the difference between well-executed social media accounts and those accounts who fail to succeed.

In this book, you'll go through 30 lessons on what matters when it comes to doing social media well. Think of these as your keys to social media. With these keys on your keychain, you can build solid relationships with friends, colleagues, associates, customers, clients....strangers...both online and off.

CHAPTER 1: HONOR

honor noun[1]

Definition of honor

1a: good name or public esteem : REPUTATION

8a: a keen sense of ethical conduct: INTEGRITY

8b: one's word given as a guarantee of performance

Honor And Content

Where honor shows itself most is within the content that you share and create. Plagiarism is both unethical and illegal. It happens when you publish anything online that isn't yours, or you don't have express permission to publish as your own. It is stealing. It applies to text, images, graphics, logos, etc. Often, the person plagiarising isn't even aware their actions are dishonorable at best or criminal at worst. For example, many people believe that all the images from the search results are free to use when they search Google for a photo. This couldn't be farther from the truth!

Honor is a pillar in the foundation of your character. Stealing is inauthentic at best and criminal at worst. You may have hundreds of thousands of followers across your social media accounts. Still, if your character isn't honorable, you have nothing. Your foundation is faulty and will eventually give out without honor, and your character will be revealed. It's not worth the risk.

We want to establish ourselves online in an honorable way. This is why investing the time and money to learn how to use social media is advantageous. Our strategic goal is to harness our online presence while we maximize the effectiveness of digital space. Tactically, we do this by sharing content that establishes us as an expert in our field. Continuous, regular posting is an excellent way to get traffic to our profiles and, eventually, websites.

> *"Google loves fresh content, and posting a blog regularly is one way to get crawled by the Google bots." Ruby Rusine[2]*

Within the context of social media, we often discuss the concept of branding. Along with other factors, character qualities have an impact on your branding. Why? Character shapes the ethics of how your social tactics will be used to achieve the goals in your overall social strategy.

There are two categories of content: created and curated. Honor and ethics apply to both.

Created Content

Created content comes out of your brain and is translated onto the paper, canvas, or back-lit screen. Ideas are never without precedent as the saying goes, "there is nothing new under the sun." However, how you present them in your own words and style is uniquely yours. Everyone has content to share, but they may not realize it. This idea is continuously reinforced in my own mind.

> *"You should be able to write 30 things down about your business. Those are your blogging topics."* Bob Watson[3]

I think it's sage advice I'm personally going to take to heart.

Curated Content

Curated Content can manifest itself in two main ways: reblogging and social sharing.

Reblogging's main appeal is that it gives you a potentially wider audience. The downside is that it essentially steals traffic, especially if it lacks proper attribution and a link to the source. Without attribution, you are claiming this work for yourself.

This is an excellent time to remind ourselves:

> *"Copying nearly all of a work, or copying its 'heart,' is less likely to be fair." Electronic Frontier Foundation[4]*

Using someone else's text on your blog without explicit permission or syndication is wrong. The insult to injury is to leave off the writer's name and link to the original work. Don't be that person. Read about this from the US Copyright Office.

Reblogging is also a way people make money with affiliate links and the like. It's the hop, skip, and a jump method of sharing, which, as a user, I find entirely annoying -- at best.

Pinterest is the ultimate in social sharing curation, especially when you pin an item from its website. Retweeting is social sharing on Twitter.

Facebook and LinkedIn allow for sharing (public and friends-only or specific circles, groups, etc.).

When you use the native sharing tools within the platform, you're pretty safe. Instagram is the only one that requires original content. The way to share with Instagram is to send a post to your story.

Social sharing is wrong when you steal photos (downloading an image, uploading an image) from *[Insert Social Network Here]* and then uploading it with or without that caption. Saying "courtesy of" does not make it okay. I've noticed this happens a lot with Buffer users and on Pinterest. It's not the tool's fault when it's users who violate both terms of service (TOS) and copyright laws.

With image use, there are a few options. You can sign up for a paid stock image service (like iStock). It's better to use images that fall under the Creative Commons license. Unsplash.com allows for attribution-free, commercial use. Canva.com also has stock photos available for free and for download.

The best bet is to always take your own photos. Building your personal stock photo library is never a bad thing. Google Photos is free for quite a bit of storage and has powerful search functions. Try searching for "red" or "tree." You'll be amazed.

Again, unless the musician, record company, or

copyright owner gives you specific permission (usually written) to use their music in your video, podcast, or other media; using such media violates copyright laws. This is why I wrote my own jingle for my videos.

CHAPTER 2: RECIPROCATION

Giant Sequoias are the most massive tree by volume and can grow to be very old. The oldest recorded Giant Sequoia tree is 3,500 years old. These giants aren't like the Lone Cypress; they live in communities. One of the reasons they can grow so tall and wide is because their root systems are interconnected. They cannot survive outside of their forest environment.

Many times, especially on Twitter, people will go through growth spurts. At first, they're happy for any followers, do somersaults for retweets, and always reply. Then, as they grow bigger, they typically abandon those growth-producing behaviors for one excuse or another.

This can leave you feeling tiny.

These giants used their Twitter community to become a 279 foot tall, 26 wide Sequoia but want to be set free from their role and responsibility in the forest. Their lack of response may harm the community and the interconnectedness they ignore. The trend is even to dump followers once they have achieved the following base they want.

Some of the trees they grew up with may feel resentment, betrayal, or just grief for the relationship loss of their former friend, the lone Sequoia, has now outgrown.

I've noticed this trend over the years. For some accounts, I'm unmotivated to continue to exist only to be their sycophant. In other words, I'm no longer willing to promote them with nothing in return continually. I may even unfollow those accounts.

Reciprocation In Relationships

Reciprocation is the basis of most relationships: I scratch your back, you scratch mine. And if this is done organically and naturally, it is a beautiful thing.

Reciprocation is the next step after a "thank you." Don't get me wrong; getting a "thank you" every once in a while is great. One of the reasons I respect Gary Vaynerchuk on Twitter is that it isn't just his philosophy to be social. Still, it continues to be his practice, though he has over two million followers.

> "No tweet left behind. Everybody who tweets has to be responded to." Gary Vanynerchuk[5]

Frankly, people should get back to the basics. That's good manners. A *thank you* or *you're welcome* is excellent, but an exchange of sharing is better for building long term relationships.

What Reciprocation Looks Like

In 2011, I felt like I was in a bit of a rut with Riggins Construction & Management, Inc.'s Twitter account[6], so I blogged about #EngageFriday[7] as a challenge to myself and others. Instead of #FF[1] [2][8] (Follow Friday) shoutouts, the premise is to go back to my five most recent followers and reply or retweet one tweet. This was a great experiment because of new seedlings of relationships that have sprouted in the form of conversations.

You may be overwhelmed. Maybe you are getting one hundred (or more) responses on Twitter a day. That can be overwhelming for sure. However, I bet you can find the time if you genuinely want to.

Ideas: How To Reciprocate Online

- Take an extra five minutes to scroll through someone's Twitter stream who retweeted you and reply or retweet to one of their tweets. This could apply to blogs, Facebook Pages, Pinterest, etc.

- Spend ten minutes in your home feed reading at other people's content. Respond appropriately to three people.

- Put people on lists so you can check out their tweets that are hours or even days old. This helps you stay in contact with the trees closest to you in the Social Forest.

- Do you have frequent retweeters or mentioners? Put them on a particular Twitter list. This will make it easier for you also to promote their content and engage with them.

- Hire an intern to manage your following, research, and posting so that you can spend time engaging.

- Use the time while you're waiting (meeting, late person at lunch, movie to start) to read over your social stream. In other words, audit your time. Figure out how you can spend it more wisely.

- If you really can't find the time to be social, don't risk losing or offending your followers; outsource your social to someone you can trust.

CHAPTER 3: RELATIONSHIPS

Home purchases. Marriages. Stock Market. No one has a problem understanding these are long-term investments. But when I bring up social media, Twitter specifically, all I hear are concerns about return on investment (ROI).

Seriously? Do you plan on starting a relationship scheming for what you can get out of it? Not only is that mindset self-centered, but it's also short-sighted. Twitter is one of the best listening tools around. Yet there is so much social failure.

> *"...sometimes, it feels like I'm the only one paying attention to others."* Amy Donohue[9]

> *"Send out your messages continuously, and*

use UPPER CASE. And lots of punctuation marks!!!!!!!!!!" Carol Stephen[10]

Return On Investment

Everyone understands how easy it is to link a tweet with a return on your investment in retail. A tweet that says "show this tweet to the cashier and get a free cookie" can be recorded and saved. When we, as consumers, love a brand, we share it with our friends. I tweet about The Real Deli and my favorite shoes, for example. All of this can be measured, quite possibly, in real-time.

But what about business to business (B2B) or commercial accounts? You can rarely point to a specific tweet that brought Customer A into your brick and mortar. It would be impossible, in many cases.

The strategy for social media in B2B relationships is different. It's about relationships, not a first-click. First click leads don't happen. Ever.

It's About Relationships

Though I tweet my heart out, put people on lists, engage, and reciprocate, I often agree with Amy's sentiment. There aren't a whole lot of people wanting to participate. But when you find them, they're like gold.

Those relationships naturally develop over time. With every interaction, conversation, your mutual trust is built up. As these new relationships usually progress, you can take them offline, as I did with Allen Buchanan[11] and Riggins Construction & Management, Inc[12].

Relationships And Branding

The feelings that people associate with your company - no matter how many touches they've had with you - is your branding. We call that feeling our emotional affinity. When you have a relationship with a person, the logo has meaning. The emblem in and of itself has little to no effect.

There's no shortcut to relationships either online or off. They take time to develop. More time and effort are required to maintain them. Given enough time, these relationships you've cultivated are like a Twitter orchard that will produce fruit. The fruit could manifest itself as friendship, referrals, or new business.

> "The best time to plant a tree is twenty years ago. The second best time is now." Chinese Proverb[13]

Strategy: A Peek Behind The Curtain

My goal, with any client's social presence and relationship building, is two-fold. I want to remain at the top of their mind when they need those services. Also, I know that eventually, the customer base will be online. I'm building the social infrastructure that helps people find my client when they Google the business. Social media is used for both validation and discovery. People will always perform searches.

Though I'm not entirely altruistic, I'm not a cat-petting, gold-ring-wearing, evil mastermind from a James Bond film.

Social Capital And Emotional Attachment

There is a gift in being an introvert; that is, introspection. Time spent thinking about why I felt too ashamed to check in on Foursquare at Subway made me realize that we subconsciously feel emotionally obligated to our friends.

Do I go to Subway in my town for a $5 footlong? No, I go to The Real Deli. I have a relationship with them. Does our IT guy stop by our office "just to say 'hello?'" Yes and no - but he knows that he keeps his brand (professional services) at the top of our mind when he comes around. Do I order keychains from some random company I find on the internet? No. My friends have a business[14]. I ordered my keychain from them.

The Bottom Line Isn't The Bottom Line

The point is that you can network from your desk, car, or anywhere in-between using social media. Though technology saves us time and frees us from the barriers of geography and time zones, it is no substitute for manners and common sense. Technology does not replace the steady, slow growth of relationships. It's a long-term investment.

CHAPTER 4: HUMILITY

As an independent musician, I found out early that no one will promote your music if you don't promote your music. Myspace was my gateway drug into this social media madness to promote my freshman CD. Yet, I find it difficult for me to switch off the self-promoting carnival barker side of my personality and demonstrate humility. I'm not above admitting that. Humility is a form of generosity; it allows us to learn, gives our ego permission to fail, and makes us teachable.

> "It is the mark of an educated mind to be able to entertain a thought without accepting it." - Aristotle[15].

If there's anything true about social media, the

only constant is change. Platforms come and go (remember when MySpace was a thing?) Trends evolve, and so do best practices (#FF[16] was once a common Twitter event but now it is considered passé, the retweet button used to be the best way to share Tweets but it has recently been called anti-social, etc.[17]) To keep up-to-date, you have to be able to entertain ideas. This is one of the reasons why I admire Gary Vaynerchuk[18]. He went all-in with Vine[19] even when people thought it was lame. Gary started using Snapchat[20], although it was (at the time) considered a platform for teenagers. In a phrase, he's a risk-taker.

> *"I'm not scared if I'm wrong, because the alternative is scarier to me... Better businesses than ours have lost by not innovating." Gary Vaynerchuk[21]*

Two more people come to mind, both of whom I know well enough online and off, who exhibit humility in both dimensions of life.

Carol Stephen

Without a doubt, Carol[22] is generous on Twitter and the Queen of all things Pinterest. That said, her blogging is phenomenal, both in content, delivery, and style. While I've been bragging that I've been featured on Yahoo Small Business a few times, Carol's posts have been picked up by Yahoo quite frequently.

I felt like a boob just doing a cursory Google search. And what blows me away is that though I'm bragging about my small accomplishment, she never says a word about herself. Instead, she congratulates me and allows me to enjoy the moment. That's humility.

Kendra Hubbard

I know that Kendra[23] rocks Twitter for #So-larChat[24]; that's obvious. But it took two years of knowing her and a road trip before I discovered that she designed and marketed the Ecoasis line of reflective roof shingles when she worked for Malarkey Roofing. Wow. She's a marketing genius whose passion for sustainability will convert even the most cynical. Now she's rocking DC trips to advocate for the solar industry among being on board of directors. I can't even keep up.

Find Those Who Inspire You

People are put in your life for a reason. Though you may disagree on philosophy, it is a shame to ignore what you can learn from others. These two women have demonstrated a generosity of spirit and genuine humility, not in pretense, but in actuality.

Truthfully, humility is a characteristic I'm humble enough to admit I haven't mastered.

Who is in your life? Have you seen humility on social media? How does humility change your social media strategy and tactics? Do you think you should alter your online behavior?

CHAPTER 5: AUTHENTICITY

Authenticity, what is it? We hear that word tossed around as an attainable attribute, but how does it affect our social media strategy? How does it alter our online behavior? Being authentic is a concept that has been used and abused like a favorite sweatshirt. It may be comfortable, but it's full of dog hair. According to Merriam-Webster[25], the third definition of authentic is "true to one's own personality, spirit, or character." The fact is that our behavior, both online and off, affects whether we are perceived as being authentic.

Authenticity And Rudeness

This must be addressed straight out of the gate. In the name of authenticity, you should not think it's okay to hurt other people's feelings. This happens both online and off. You can be a helpful person on social media by giving constructive criticism. If you do it well, it will resonate as authentic.

People use authenticity as an excuse for rude comments. A real person once said, to me, *"That lipstick looks terrible on you. Just being honest."* I hadn't asked for her input and I liked the lipstick just fine. You both can and should edit your comments online - and in person. Inhibition is what saves friendships. If you're not convinced, your extra credit assignment is to watch the video[26] by Derek Sivers called: A real person, a lot like you." It's in the footnotes.

Authenticity And First Impressions

I rarely meet new people on any platform other than Twitter. When I come upon a new follower or person during a Twitter Chat or recommendation from a mutual friend, I check out their profile. Just like in real life, first impressions count.

For example, suppose an account solely publishes tweets from their same Facebook content. In that case, I presume they rarely check their Twitter account. So why bother following? If their avatar is an egg or if they have a risque biography, they are most likely spam. I can apply the same red flags we have in real life to online behavior.

> *"But I ask you...are any of you rockin' the 'Snuggie' on a first date? Are you sporting the grey sweats from Wal-Mart and the fleece boots when he knocks on your front door? Are you wearing the red flannel shirt that you love, but is seriously ten years too old? Of course not! (At least, you shouldn't - BTW.) Then you shouldn't do the same at work. It's not a breach of authenticity to dress to impress. The same goes with our words."*
> *Rommel Anacan[27]*

Authenticity And Personality

I tend to agree with Stacy Garcia and Amy Don-ohue; the best way to be authentic on social media is to let your personality shine through. This can be a challenge at first. Like any writer, finding your voice takes time and practice. Yes, Tweeting is writing. You have to be concise and interesting in a limited amount of characters. Personality endears you to people and makes you stand out. In-person, the first impression is created the moment you first encounter someone. Online it's with a new follower.

Stacy Garcia (@CabinetMakers) makes a great point. The test of your authenticity online is when the relationship moves offline.

Your online behavior matters, which brings me to scheduling tweets - a heated debate more often than not.

Authenticity And Scheduling

Scheduling and automation are different. I schedule tweets for clients, but no more than two weeks ahead. Automating tweets can get you in a mess of trouble.

"There is no such thing as automated engagement. There is no such thing as programmed authenticity." Scott Stratten[28]

On the flip side, I went to Syed Balkhi's Time Management talk one year at WordCamp OC. He lives by Buffer and other scheduling apps. His approach makes sense, too. So what's the big deal? Why should you care?

Potential Problems With Scheduling Tweets

- People respond to your tweets (comments or retweets), and you're not there to continue the conversation. This is the big challenge of pushing out content on social media too far ahead of time.
- A friend died a couple of years ago, and his account kept tweeting because of automation he set up. It was awkward at best and eerie at worst.
- National and local tragedies happen. You need to be online to stop scheduled tweets.
- Everyone has schedules, meetings, and offline times. We get that you're busy. There has to be some middle ground.

There is a hybrid approach that is authentic. I've concluded that it is best that I only schedule tweets for myself for the day, and only when I'll be online checking for responses. That's a great compromise. For clients, I schedule two weeks out.

Authenticity And Programmed Responses

Did you know that you can automate retweets? I stumbled upon it because an account was not only retweeting conversation fragments but when I finally called them out on Twitter, they retweeted that, too. This is inauthentic and poor branding for many reasons.

Seriously? If you do not have time to retweet things from your lists or home feed (better with a comment), then maybe Twitter just isn't for you. Yes, I said it. Maybe you should quit Twitter altogether. Remember, the point is to build relationships.

Authenticity And Branding

From a branding perspective, authenticity is what differentiates you from the other guy. A little bit of personality, your manners, the way you engage with your audience all build your identity. Suppose there is a difference between your audience's perception (branding) and reality (poor customer service, ignoring tweets). In that case, somebody may label you as inauthentic.

There are a plethora of blog posts about social media fails. This is the layman's way of pointing out inauthentic behavior.

Authenticity And Humanity

Social media is social. That is a basic fact that will never change. And there are indeed only 24 hours in a day, 60 minutes in an hour, and so on. Time is a precious resource we often take for granted. But should our relationships suffer to save a few seconds? At what point does automation dehumanize us?

True, deepened, and connected relationships are critical to our sense of humanity and belonging. All of us, by biological default, want to be recognized within our social groups. In fact, "love and belonging" ranks third in Maslow's hierarchy of needs. All of us want to fit in. We all crave attention and purpose.

At some point, to stay authentic, we'll have to start treating social media as the place where we can find connectedness.

When someone asks us a question in the physical world, we only have mere seconds to reply before the moment is lost, and the subject is changed. Yet, on social media, we feel that it is okay to wait for days to reply to people or never respond at all.

CHAPTER 6: THE GOLDEN RULE

Who remembers first grade? Among stretching exercises, snack time, recess, and learning to read with Dick & Jane, there was a sign way, way high up on the classroom wall. "Do Unto Others As You Would Have them Do Unto You." Do you remember that? Is it taught anymore? Lately, it seems like the internet doesn't embrace this fundamental axiom of human relations. Even Ted Rubin started a Twitter account to remind people to Just be Nice.

A Word On Kindness

Kindness is the bonding agent that allows two people with diverse interests and opinions to become friends. It's such a simple, basic concept. It's a wonder that we forget. Yet, our fast-paced society with blue-backlit screens has perhaps de-sensitized us. Have we been stripped of our sense of dignity and manners in the name of authenticity? Has "keeping it real" been an excuse for brutal honesty? At what point does this cyberbullying break down all meaningful communication?

In "How We're Talking, Like Today[29]" from On Point with Tom Ashbrook, the panel discusses verbal tee-ups. Essentially, we permit ourselves to be rude with phrases like "To be honest," "just sayin'" and "bless her heart." Maybe Derek Sivers is right. Maybe being behind a computer dehumanizes us to the point that we forget who is on the other side. "At the end of every computer is a real person, a lot like you." Derek Sivers You, too, can be a jerk.

Yep. I screwed up, too.

I talked to a pal a few months back and thought Scott Stratten's UnPodcast was too long. Though a fan (read 2 of his books, attended a live event, read his blog, etc.) I had hoped it would be shorter and more easily consumable. So, I tweeted that, not thinking he might have a search set up for "UNPod-cast," and he called me out on it. "what does the length have to do with the 'Un'?" He was right to do so. I apologized and learned a valuable lesson that day.

He has some good advice on how to deal with "trolls," too. It's effortless to engage in light criticism to outright name-calling on social media because it seems like it will never come back to us. But it could come back to bite you. Would knowing that make a difference? It did for me.

"Weekly reminder to ignore the haters. You're not the Jackass Whisperer." Scott Stratten[30]

Don't Look For Trouble

It was an ordinary day yesterday. My WordPress app told me my stats were heating up. Excited, I looked at my stats and saw that my post "Why I Don't Use Twitter's Retweet Button" had gotten lots of hits, but my mentions column in Twitter was dry. Which, I thought, was curious. Wanting to thank the person who shared my post, I searched Twitter for the post's URL. I found this:

Devang Desai @DesaiDevang · Jan 28
Ladies and gentlemen of the jury, may I present history's greatest monster: youtoocanbeaguru.wordpress.com/2013/03/18/why...

Details ↰ Reply ⟲ Retweet ★ Favorited ⬆ Buffer ⬇ Pocket ••• More

Bridget Willard
@YouTooCanBeGuru

Dear @DesaiDevang ,
"Monster" is a bit strong.
But thanks for tweeting out my link. I appreciate it.

↰ Reply 🗑 Delete ★ Favorite ⬆ Buffer ••• More

RETWEET
1

0:15 AM - 28 Jan 2014 from Industry, CA

Reply to @DesaiDevang

JB **Justin Bourne** @jtbourne · Jan 28
@YouTooCanBeGuru @DesaiDevang "Internet villain" would've sufficed, D.

Details ↰ Reply ⟲ Retweet ★ Favorite ⬆ Buffer ••• More

My mind was blown. Monster? Wow. Not only was this person not following me, but he also didn't even know me. It was as if my post told people to kill their childhood dog or burn their deceased grandpa's baseball card collection. First, I was mad. Then hurt. Then I began to doubt. Did I tell people they were doing something wrong? Was I too offensive? But the truth is that you will, by default, have dissenters when you take a position.

Having extra time, I decided to engage, under the premise that a "soft answer turns away wrath." I replied, saying that the term seemed harsh but thanked him for tweeting my post. And one tweet led me to another, which led to another. I probably shouldn't have "fed the trolls," but maybe using a soft answer was a way to be truly authentic. I'm a real person, I'm not a computer, and my intention was simply to clarify this accusation.

CHAPTER 7: RESPONSIBILITY

Do you ever consider the role of responsibility and digital space? Or does it seem like the internet is just fast and loose and wild and carefree? As a (social media) creator, you have a certain level of responsibility if you want your social efforts to maintain some semblance of success.

As defined by Merriam-Webster[32], responsibility is "the state of being the person who caused something to happen, a duty or task that you are required or expected to do, and/or something that you should do because it is morally right, legally required, etc." When populating your social media accounts with your content (or any content, really), you are causing things to happen. Therefore, you should honorably fulfill those things expected of you. This includes refraining from anything that is or can be interpreted as illegal, hateful, unkind, ungracious, etc. This responsibility thing isn't a mystery.

Responsibility To Create

The primary reason to put yourself out there is to gain a following and audience with whom you can share your experience, knowledge, and insight. If you're artistic, take photos, sketch, shoot video, or make compelling graphics. Musicians can compose, and writers publish blogs. The more you post original content, the better you will become and, therefore, increase the likelihood that somebody will share your content in their social circles.

Responsibility To Respond

Recently, at a local mastermind, someone stated that Facebook Pages have little to no engagement. Being the yin to his yang, I raised my hand. I've commented many times on tons of pages where the page admin has not responded. Just crickets. And, unless you own a pet store and sell them to frog owners, crickets are not the desired response. You, the page admin (yes, you), have a responsibility to respond promptly.

Responsibility To Reciprocate

Reciprocation goes beyond good manners; it is the most underused tool in the social toolbox. When you take the time to find a tweet or two to share from a new follower or frequent retweeter, I'd be willing to bet that you will win their loyalty. This tactic kills two birds with the one proverbial stone: you've shared content other than your own, and you've encouraged a new relationship.

Responsibility To Moderate

You absolutely cannot let trolls ruin your digital space with their type-written graffiti. That said, all people, even non-troll humans, get mad. Anger motivates people to lash out on social media. This is an excellent reason to stay on top of notifications, especially during business hours and/or weekends, if you are a retail establishment. Having the wisdom and discernment of when and how to reply (public or private response) separates good brands from great ones. A speedy response can totally turn sentiment around in your favor. An excellent example of this is Scott Stratten's post "How Delta's Tweet Saved the Brand Day."

Responsibility To Inspire

Apple took the responsibility to inspire others very seriously: they put the user experience at the top of their priority list. Think about how easy it is to use all of their products. They focus on what is intuitive for the end-users and dismiss everything else. Need proof? Just look around at all the baby boomers and senior citizens enjoy using their iPhones and iPads. And we all know way too many two-year-olds who can play iPhone games!

> *"Our DNA is as a consumer company - for that individual customer who's voting thumbs up or thumbs down. That's who we think about. And we think that our job is to take responsibility for the complete user experience. And if it's not up to par, it's our fault, plain and simple." ~ Steve Jobs[33]*

Your posts, the content you decide to share, or create can inspire your digital audience. Inspiration can change behavior. If we're honest, behavior change is one of the primary concerns of a business - especially buying behavior. In the case of the Chip and Applebee's Relationship (hat tip to Carol Stephen - Your Social Media Works), the customer engaged with Applebee's and vice versa. It seems the friendship escalated and is now inspiring many others, presumably this audience as well.

I asked my tweeps what they thought the relationship in social media is with regard to responsibility.

Bridget Willard
@YouTooCanBeGuru

Last week at #SMMOC we touched on responsibility as it applies to social media.
How do you think it applies?
Use tag #SocialResponsibility

9:12 AM · Jan 8, 2014 · Twitter for iPhone

Here are their responses.

Amy Donohue
@TheFabulousOne

Use your Page as the Page to like and comment on other posts. #socialresponsibility

10:37 AM · Jan 8, 2014 · TweetDeck

Amy Donohue
@TheFabulousOne

Like Pages back that liked yours! #socialresponsibility

10:36 AM · Jan 8, 2014 · TweetDeck

Amy Donohue
@TheFabulousOne

Remember to check your @ mentions to respond.
#payattention #socialresponsibility

10:36 AM · Jan 8, 2014 · TweetDeck

Amy Donohue
@TheFabulousOne

Make sure to thank people for a RT! #SocialResponsibility

10:35 AM · Jan 8, 2014 · TweetDeck

tracy
@tracycopy

If a person takes the time to respond to 1 of your tweets, then respond to them in a timely manner.
#SocialResponsibility

11:34 AM · Jan 8, 2014 · TweetDeck

Kirti D.
@DiyaMarketing

If someone comments on a FB post or responds to your tweet--respond back! #SocialMedia is about engagement, after all. #SocialResponsibility

12:54 PM · Jan 8, 2014 · Twitter Web Client

RUBY 💯| Social Media Content+Metrics ✴
@SocialSMktg

#SocialResponsibility I regularly visit other pages that took the time to visit mine. I follow their digital trail (likes & comments).

3:32 PM · Jan 8, 2014 · Twitter Web Client

CHAPTER 8: COURAGE

This book has focused heavily on strategy and its relation to our character. With this post, we'll focus on courage. What does courage have to do with social media? It is the lack of courage that keeps people from either fully engaging or prevents them from experimentation. It does take a bit of bravado to pull off the humor and some courage to try new things. My friends often describe me as the "penguin who jumps off of the ice first," but that's just with social media. The truth is, I usually don't try uncomfortable things without a little prompting - either internal or external.

At a meetup, a new attendee confessed she was worried she wasn't keeping up with the trends and wanted to try [insert new, fancy, social platform here] but didn't know-how. The men responded with very logical answers about making time, putting it on your daily agenda, and fitting it into your schedule.

Sounds right, but my woman's intuition kicked in. Raising my hand in a very non-powerful, meek way, I waited patiently for my turn to speak. I turned around, looked her in the eye, and said, "It sounds to me like you're motivated but afraid. Maybe you need [the social media version of] a walking buddy." Boom. I saw in her eyes that I had hit the nail on its proverbial head. Fear is a horrible, silent predator that cripples to the point of defeat, forcing us to retreat into a cave. Fear leaves us feeling powerless to change the things we want to improve in our lives.

Walking Buddy

Do you have a mentor? How about a support network? Friends or mentors who encourage us are essential parts of our lives. In the digital age, we work more independently and feel like we don't need others (working at home being one of those trends). Companies like Yahoo have realized that the company suffers in the innovation department when their employees work at home.

Why? It can be a lack of creativity. Throughout school, I despised group projects. It always came down to me being the one who does all of the work. What suffers in individual work is brainstorming, checking ideas, conflict (it can be a good thing), and the support you get when a concept clicks. I learned to brainstorm with my coworkers about company blog posts (how else will you learn about stormwater retention?). I bounced ideas off of my husband, who was a well-educated, open-minded person.

Above that, I have a blogging version of a walking buddy - my oft-quoted, life-long, best ROI of Twitter, friend, Carol Stephen. Either online or off, we'll bounce ideas around like brightly-colored plastic balls in a bounce house, allowing ourselves to be silly. It has been a fruitful relationship. I challenged her to blog in the first place; she challenges me to blog more often. This whole series has come about because of her encouragement.

External Courage

Encouragement. Yes. We all need it. Do you think about what the word encourage means? It means to give courage - to fill with courage. Each of us has the power to encourage someone else in a way that will help them succeed. The bequeathing of courage can be done both online and off. Frankly, praise should be public, and correction should be private. My think-tank does this. There is no way I'd be who I am today without their support (encouragement).

My friend Pam Aungst describes how a "Secret Group" on Facebook changed her life:

> *"What happened after that is indescribable. This group of women has become WAY more than just 'Twitter friends.' We have personally and professionally gotten to know each other on a deeper level than ever expected. We share personal joys and issues, as well as professional successes and challenges. These women feel like family to me."*
> *Pam Aungst[34]*

Family. Yes. That feeling comes because of acceptance. Acceptance is what makes people feel safe enough to share their fears. This is why it is so important to be involved in a peer group.

Internal Courage

Some things are comfortable; we don't need cour-age for what is easy. But when faced with a chal-lenge, we need to tap into and conjure up the con-fidence that comes from inner strength - courage.

"My own definition of confidence is 'being there.' This means being in the moment and acting with intention, not distracted by second thoughts or being 'in your head.' Not listening to your inner critics or assuming what others are thinking of you, judging or presupposing 'their' reaction in-stead of just moving forward—and confidently."
James Victore[35]

That's a kind of internal courage life-hack. Be in the moment. Don't worry about what people will think. Just create.

As social media strategists, we aim to either find out what people think or shape what people think. You can't start the first draft, however, until you open up your laptop. You have to begin by starting.

Inner courage is made up of both faith and experi-ence and is mixed with our determination.

Do we think of brave people as naturally brave?

Maybe. But maybe it's just sheer determination. You know, like the ant who moved the rubber tree plant. It could be your outlook. Do you have ant's "high hopes?"

Faith can start externally but must be nurtured internally.

Fake It 'Til You Become It

In Amy Cuddy's "Your body language shapes who you are" TED Talk, she describes how people actually feel more in control and courageous after changing their posture for just two minutes.

> "We are also influenced by our non-verbals: our thoughts and our feelings and our physiology. ... When you pretend to be powerful, you are more likely to feel powerful." Amy Cuddy[36]

Through the 21 minute talk, she gives her own story of transforming from feeling powerless to feeling powerful and changing the way we think about ourselves.

> "Don't fake it 'til you make it. Fake it until you become it." Amy Cuddy[37]

Everyone, at some point, at some level, experiences fear. Naturally, that will translate into tweets and posts on social media as people often share their anxieties.

How To Respond To Those Tweets

This is your defining moment. This is where your character expresses itself into tactics. Will you reply with a word of encouragement? Will you start an argument? It's up to you. You can help them escape that dark pit of fear, or you can walk away. Your response defines who you are - it defines your character.

CHAPTER 9: CONVERSATION

"A single conversation across the table with a wise man is better than ten years mere study of books." ~ Henry Wadsworth Longfellow[38]

W hat role does a conversation have in social media?

If you are of the persuasion, as I am, that social media is about conversational relationships, then the art thereof is one of social media's primary requisites. People generally understand how to comment and converse blog-style on Facebook, Instagram, and Google Plus. But with Twitter, the syntax seems to leave even experienced users perplexed. It's funny to me how frequently I am asked how one starts a conversation on Twitter. The answer is always the same.

"You start a conversation on Twitter the same way you do in real life."

Hold that thought. Let's first discuss the retweet button and your social strategy.

The Retweet Button: A Conversation Inhibitor

It seems that a retweet is commonly accepted as a substitute for "thank you" or "you're welcome." And this is why the conversation is stopped. I am pretty famous (or infamous depending on whether you agree with me) for my opinion about Twitter's Retweet Button. But it comes down to two major reasons for me: manners and conversation.

To make my point, I tweeted:

I liked this reply:

B.C. Kowalski
@BC_Kowalski

Replying to @YouTooCanBeGuru

@YouTooCanBeGuru In real life, Twitter itself would be randomly saying things and hoping someone replies.

10:19 AM · Jan 20, 2014 · Twitter for iPhone

Though I do not entirely agree with him, keep his thought in mind while I digress to strategy.

Strategy: Define Your Why

Strategy determines tactics. If your primary purpose on Twitter is to opine and to be known for such, then you'll like being retweeted. You can collect those stats like baseball cards, showing them off when your friends and family come to visit. Being retweeted in this scenario is a good thing (for the opiner). However, if you are the person retweeting, you get little to nothing out of your effort.

If your purpose of being on Twitter is to meet new people, then the conversation tactic is the one for you.

Let's go back to B.C. Kowalski's thoughts. Is Twitter full of randomly blurted out phrases and questions? Are people venting to no specific audience? If no one reads a tweet in the social media forest, does it exist?

He makes a philosophical point. True, one person couldn't possibly read every tweet in their timeline. But what about the tweets you see right now? Can you spend two-three minutes reading those (excluding the linked content)? Yes, right now in the home feed. Go take a look. I'll wait. Without scrolling more than three times, is there one tweet that you can reply to? If the answer is yes, then you've just done the equivalent of walking over to a person at a party, perhaps so shy that they're hiding behind the cheese tray, and started a conversation. It's true that if we were taking this analogy quite literally, the cheese plate hiding person is also talking to themselves, but I digress. Let's stick with the premise.

When you read a tweet, you have the choice, dare I say power, to reply. You can make that one person (or group of two) feel more comfortable.

"Twitter is a party that your neighbor's brother-in-law's mother is having. You won't know ANYONE when you get there. How are you going to get through it? Easy. You start jumping in on conversations and learning about others, so you make friends. Talk about what THEY are talking about, and, eventually, they will ask about YOU."
Amy Donohue[39]

Strategy: Start A Twitter Conversation

Being the cliche introvert, my husband always told me to ask questions at parties. "People love to talk about themselves." It's true. You can start a conversation on Twitter in one of two ways: ask a question or comment on a tweet.

In Carol Stephen's "Social Media Conversation Starters," she advises us to make the conversation about the other person.

> *"Don't be waiting for a break in the conversation so you can talk about yourself. Let the other person lead and be willing to be surprised by listening."*

Bookmark "101 Conversation Starters," and refer to it often. Eventually, it will come naturally!

Case in point: Today, I tweeted my Foursquare check-in. It resulted in 13 replies with three people because Chef Ivan Flowers asked me a straightforward question: "How do you get your burger?"

Chef Ivan[40] has a strong social media game!

Strategy: Tweet A Question In A Reply

You can ask questions about a user's bio, which is made more comfortable if you have commonalities. For example, if someone's bio says they live in Fresno and you went to Fresno State, you can ask about the school, weather, restaurants, etc. Mix a question with a bit of empathy for the best impact.

Examples (Twitter handles are fictitious):
- Hey, @Fresno_Guy, I used to go to Fresno State. How are the Bulldogs doing?
- @Fresno_Guy Oh man. I remember Central Valley winters. How's the Tulle Fog treating you?
- If you have a sport or sports team in common, you can ask for their opinion on recent coaching decisions or whom they think will win the next event.

Curiosity also fuels conversation. If you find a hot air balloon pilot but have never been in a hot air balloon, ask them about their passion.

Examples:
- @BeautifulBalloon Where is your favorite place to fly?
- @BeautifulBalloon What is your favorite festival?

Strategy: Comment On A Tweet

The comment tweet is my favorite form of retweeting (RT). When you see a tweet that sparks your interest, copy/paste the tweet's unique URL, with a comment in front. This method keeps some of the context intact. Then you wait for them to respond.

Disclaimer: people often do not respond right away (sometimes, they never do.) Don't let that bother you - just keep on working your social media strategy!

Try starting conversations on Twitter for a week or two. Spend five to ten minutes a day looking at your lists or home feed and pressing the reply button. You never know what you might learn or whom you may meet!

CHAPTER 10: CONTENT

In real estate, you often hear the mantra, "Location, Location, Location." In many ways, this also applies to digital real estate: "Content, Content, Content." Thoughts drive social media. Thoughts become ideas. Ideas become action. Commonalities and relationships are forged because of thoughts and similar experiences. Consistently sharing content (your thoughts, ideas, and action) will set you apart.

When You Have Nothing To Say

Have you ever thought to yourself that everything meaningful has already been said? Maybe it has. I'm sure there is another blogging series or posts that are better than this one. But this is my creation, and the words come out in my voice.

Believe me, you have ideas. You have your style, and you have a voice. You can add value to the world. Are you worried you'll just state the obvious? Maybe the obvious isn't that obvious.

> "Everybody's ideas seem obvious to them. Maybe what's obvious to me is amazing to someone else." Derek Sivers[41]

Where To Get Ideas

You know more than you think. Do your customers frequently ask the same questions? Do you find that you explain processes often with a subconscious script? You may need to ask yourself questions or respond to prompts or brainstorm with a friend or coworker. But you have ideas.

Also, lots of content creators like Tess Wittler give their ideas for free. I recently downloaded her free ebook[42], "52 Content Ideas for Residential Contractors," which has given me plenty to think about, especially since the ideas are arranged by topic.

Blogging Is Like Making Meatloaf

Every day in this country, someone prepares a meal for their family to consume around the proverbial dinner table. At the same time, they catch up with each other. Think Norman Rockwell. Now think of a dish that has been served from coast to coast in America since you can remember. Did you think of meatloaf?

How many meatloaf recipes do you think exist? I googled "meatloaf recipe," and there were over seven million results. SEVEN MILLION. How can there be seven million recipes when meatloaf's basic ingredients are ground meat, an egg, and breadcrumbs? Yet almost everyone I know has their twist on this classic dish. My aunt uses steel-cut Irish oats. My friend Steve uses turkey meat and mustard powder. My mom makes a birthday cake out of it! Take the standard meatloaf and make it your own. Dress up the potatoes. Serve it with a salad. Make your lemonade. Your style makes the dish your own.

That's how content creation is. We all have a unique set of experiences that influence how we see the world. That perspective gives us a voice in the content creation world. Are you going to stop making meatloaf because it has been overplayed? Will your family be denied the meatloaf experience because now you're a shy cook? No. That is absurd. You have a hungry audience waiting right at your dinner table. No matter how you make your meatloaf, if you consistently feed your hungry meatloaf fans, they'll keep coming back for more.

The same is true with the readers of your content. They read your content because they like YOU.

Types Of Content You Can Create

- A tweet is a sentence or two.
- A post can be paragraphs long.
- A blog post can be 300-800 words.
- An ebook can be 10-100 pages.
- Other content forms include song, video, photography, graphic art, the canvas.

The content you create is only limited by your imagination. All of that content can be shared using your social media platform of choice. Roll up your sleeves, pick a platform, and get to work.

CHAPTER 11: PASSION

As the local guru to my crew, I'm often asked how-to questions. This time, my niece introduced me to a family friend while we were in the buffet line at a shower. This beautiful soul was curious about how to use a blog to promote her new book. This silver-haired, tender-hearted woman had written a book. Sadly, she didn't feel she could manage writing a blog. I looked her in the eye and said, "You have something to say. You can add value to the world." Her eyes began to well up, and her face changed entirely. She believed me. She believed in herself.

It was a teachable moment for her and an inspiration to me. In between the requisite shower games, we continued our conversation. The more we brainstormed, the more energized I became. Driving home, I realized this is my passion. There's a part of me that will always be a teacher. I love it when someone's brain clicks. You can see it on their face.

Passion

Whether you're a speaker and it adds believability to your talk (see my video here) or whether you're a writer, you must tap into your passion. Here's what Ralph Waldo Emerson had to say about the relationship between enthusiasm and success.

> *"Enthusiasm is one of the most powerful engines of success. When you do a thing, do it with all your might. Put your whole soul into it. Stamp it with your own personality. Be active, be energetic, be enthusiastic and faithful, and you will accomplish your object. Nothing great was ever achieved without enthusiasm." - Ralph Waldo Emerson[43]*

Conveying passion, either in person or on video, is relatively easy. As Exhibit A, I give you Gary Vaynerchuk's video[44] "Why You Need to Subscribe to My Channel." Gary is passionate and enthusiastic with his tone, inflection, facial expressions, body language, and word choice:

> *"My grandmother is crying because of your lack of your subscribing to my YouTube channel."* Gary Vaynerchuk[45]

That's emotionally persuasive.

Introverts And Passion

No. Passion is not exclusive to extroverts. You can be a person who thinks deeply, needs time alone to recharge, and still engages in person and the written word. Because we're people, we all have passion.

Passion And Fear

What holds us back? Fear? I'd have to say that
a lack of courage is our biggest enemy when it
comes to our passion. Don't allow fear to stop you.

Find Your Passion

Start asking yourself questions. These are the things you want to write and speak about.If you don't trust your self-evaluation, ask a trusted friend.

- What floats your boat?
- What gets your brain going?
- What are you opinionated about?
- What makes you angry, sad, upset?

Passion And Career Choice

Not all of us have the luxury of quitting our day job to pursue our passion, but that doesn't mean we cannot nurture it. That's precisely what I've done in my blog. Heck, even Superman had a day job as Clark Kent, Batman as Bruce Wayne. Our hobbies may never lead to careers, but that doesn't make them any less valuable.

On the flip side, many people have quit their day jobs to pursue their passions. Read "Internet Marketing as a Career: Where to Start?" by Pam Angust.

CHAPTER12: CONSISTENCY

"Consistency is the last refuge for the un-imaginative." ~ *Oscar Wilde[46]*

D o you debate blogging based on consistency versus inspiration? Are you a slave to the editorial calendar? Do you fear the impending, un-avoidable lack of quality that only comes with consistency? Yet consistency is vital to our skill-set. Like any skill, you must practice your writing. That reason alone, regardless of consideration for Google's search math or serving your audience, is enough to compel me to publish more regularly.

The Confession

I admit that when I started blogging, I was selfish. I wrote when I felt compelled or was asked a question.

You may also have the excuse that *Life Happens*. "At the end of the day, blogs, Twitter, Facebook are just sites. Sometimes the world is more important than the digital one we live in." Scott Stratten, "Frequently Futile: How Often Should You Blog"

Self care is important. If you sit at your computer and start crying, then you've not had enough downtime. Maybe every week is too much. I have tons of peers who publish once a month. That's what works for them. Do that if you can.

If you want to be taken seriously as a business, you have to treat your business like your best client. This is what I began doing. I publish nearly every Friday and have for a year or two. I've also hired John Locke of lockedownseo.com to do some keyword research and give me headlines and topics to build my cornerstone content.

We all struggle. Be kind to yourself. But be realistic, too. The solution is what separates us from our competition.

The Solution

Even as a full-time freelancer, consistency in blogging was my biggest nemesis. To solve that problem, I had to put myself in my clients' shoes. What would I tell them?

I'd say that my writing should be like my most important client. Right? So, I blocked out two hours on my calendar every Friday and called it "blogging time." I don't take client calls on Fridays and it's right on my Google Calendar nagging me every week.

As a reward, I am free to take the rest of the day off, go on an outing with friends, join happy hour, or just stay at home and order a pizza.

It's hard. But yes. This is our business. No one can care about it more than we do.

Strategy Prognosis

What seems to be my problem? I'm focused (this blog is only about social media). Isn't that enough?

Part of my problem was that I treated my blog as a vehicle of convenience rather than a place to build a community. How so? The bulk of my posts are responsive. That is, when someone asks a question, I answer it in a post. I think that if I'm going to help one person, I may as well put it out there for the rest of the world, right? When asked that same question, I send a link to the relevant post.

Here's the problem with that writing strategy. My past self was an employee. Since 2017, I've been freelancing full time. Getting there meant I had to change my behavior. I attended conferences, Meetups, and have collaborated with peers. You have to leave your safe zone.

Write-Hack

One trick that helps me stay in focus, besides my Google Calendar appointment, is writing a series of blog posts about a specific topic. Deciding to write a series puts me in a state of mind to micro-focus.

For example, for the blog posts that became this book, I had to ask and answer this fundamental question: What are the crucial factors in being social on Twitter? Those answers became the titles to the Keys to Being Social series which is now this book (edited and updated, of course). Once you get the hang of thinking about your content in terms of a series of focused blog posts, the rhythm and cadence of publishing your content will start to flow naturally.

For Riggins Construction, I wrote a whole series on how office work is like housework. People loved the analogies and the "easy to integrate in your life right now" tips. Back in the day, they were called helpful hints. Today the vogue word is life-hack. When it is work-related, work-hack is more appropriate. Can you ask yourself a global question then answer it in steps? If your answer is yes, then you can create a blog series.

The Dead-End Draft Folder

I used to start drafts in there and come back to add, delete, rewrite, but then they would just be there, staring back at me like puppies I'd abandoned at the pound. I could hear them speak to me. The drafted posts asked why I didn't give them attention. I felt a sense of guilt. In an attempt to avert those feelings, I simply didn't return.

How did I overcome it? I started using iCloud Notes. It's simple. I can pull out my phone, type in an idea, and access it via iCloud(dot)com anytime. I'm composing this ebook using iCloud Notes right now. It brings quite a bit of satisfaction to finish my writing in iCloud Notes, copy/paste the content into my mobile-friendly blog post editor, add a photo to the post, proofread one last time, publish the blog post and then delete the iCloud Note!

I also began to embrace Google Docs. It's helpful to be able to use voice typing[47] to get what you want out -- if touching the keyboard paralyzes you.

CHAPTER 13: SPONTANEITY

"Humor is a spontaneous, wonderful bit of an outburst that just comes. It's unbridled, it's unplanned, it's full of surprises." — Erma Bombeck[48]

Social media seems to be obsessed with planning. There's no harm in planning. Some posts can be keyword analyzed, penciled into your editorial calendar, and scheduled three months in advance.

The problem with planning is, well, life happens. Suppose you cannot respond to life events in real-time. In that case, you're missing out on a big (often-times fun!) part of the spontaneous culture that embodies online social media. If you plan, leave a little room for the day-to-day life events that cannot be predicted, planned, and prepped. In many ways, planning gives us room for spontaneity. You want to have a well prepared and consistent social media content schedule - but leave a little room for some fun.

Dunking In The Dark

As far as big brands go, Oreo takes the cake on spontaneity. I realize it's old news by now, but the timing was perfect. I saw their tweet before my husband could come in from the other room to tell me the power went out.

I know what you're thinking. You're a real person - not a big brand like Oreo. You do not have a staff of social media marketers just waiting for a pop-culture fumble to leverage as marketing material to promote their iconic cookie.

So, how can spontaneity (real-time marketing) translate into your life?

Personal Spontaneity

Think for a moment. What memories survive when you recollect gatherings with friends? Are they the planned ones? No, it's unexpected moments that people remember. It's when you accidentally photobomb your friend's Instagram Live marriage proposal, and the live stream goes wild with emoji-reactions! It's when you're looking for a conference, and you suddenly say,

"I see hipsters. We must be here," followed by an eruption of laughter only comparable to a Mount St. Helens eruption.

Make A Meme Of Yourself

Humor takes a bit of personal courage and humility, especially if you intend upon being the butt of your joke.

Being Irish, I wore green for St. Patrick's Day and posted a selfie. My pal, Linda Snell, commented about how she felt compelled to add a rainbow and shamrocks. Being in a quirky mood, I had my coworker take a photo of me, hands held out flat so that she could add said rainbow. I posted it on Facebook with the challenge. It was so funny, but my coworkers said it was missing a unicorn (I always say 'unicorns and rainbows' as a generic happy place) and a leprechaun.

Five minutes later, she posted this. Of course, I made that my cover photo.

Then my friend Peter Woolvett joined in and posted. User-generated content (UGC) is like gold to marketers. I was willing to make a fool out of myself for a few laughs. It allowed us to exercise our creativity, bond through laughter, and entertain others. As a bonus, it became fodder for this section. Win-Win.

CHAPTER 14: COMMON SENSE

The key to your online privacy is common sense. In every other area of our lives, we have levels of intimacy, and certain people are never allowed to have our most private information. Do you leave your front door unlocked and let just anyone walk in? No. That'd be ridiculous. When your friends come for dinner, do you give them access to every room? Can your neighbor look in your underwear drawer? Then why do you let everyone in all of your digital spaces? Dinner guests don't get access to our tax returns, so why are you letting someone you just met on Twitter be your friend on Facebook?

Define Your Safe Place

The first thing you need to do is decide which network will be a safe place. This is the place where you allow yourself to be the most open. For me, that's Facebook.

Back in my Mafia Wars days (yes, I got wrapped up in that), I let every Tom, Dick, and Harry be my friend. I needed them to be my friend so that I could advance through the levels. After I quit that (and subsequently the rest of the social-obligation games), I slowly unfriended my former mafiosos.

Define Your Gateway

Your gateway is where you decide you'll meet new people, deepen relationships, and maybe take them to another level, possibly offline. For me, that's Twitter. My primary personality on Twitter has over 14,000 followers. On Facebook (my safe place), I have around 800. I can count on one hand, the people I've "met on Facebook." Twitter is my gateway for the general public, if you will.

If the relationship progresses, I may allow them on other networks, but they're always trial-based. If there are any red flags, they get unfollowed or unfriended. That's why the filtering works.

Sidebar: Auto Direct Messages On Twitter

People use direct messages for many reasons. Some people I've talked to think it's a time-saving "thank you" device. More often than not, I'm sorry to say, some will perceive direct messages as too-much-too-soon, rude behavior, and/or spam.

Sending an Auto-DM to your new follower to friend you on Facebook, connect on Linkedin, and/or sign up for your blog is like expecting to shake a new person's hand. Still, when you hold out your hand, they push their business card right in your face - an inch from your eyes.

Seriously, reconsider. Social Oomph is one of the primary Auto DM platforms. You can opt-out by following the directions in this tweet.

SocialOomph Opt-Out
@optmeout

Process to opt-out: 1) Follow me, 2) Wait for follow back, 3) Send me a DM, 4) Unfollow me. Must be done in that order.

9:18 AM · Feb 12, 2009 · Twitter Web Client

79 Retweets   **101** Likes

Define Your Intimacy Progression

This step requires introspection. While thinking about my subconscious filters, I made the Relationship Pyramid. I have not included EVERY social network, but you get the gist of it.

The Relationship Pyramid is like a funnel. The widest part at the top is the gateway; the bottom is the safe place. In between are the major networks and where they lie in this funnel of friendship.

This intimacy filter is my main reason for not auto cross-posting to every network. For the sake of convenience, my Twitter followers are not going to see my no-makeup photos with my dogs. That's too intimate for the general population.

Your Posts, Your Reputation

Yes, we are savvier and more open these days with the invasion of online marketing and peer pressure to share. In many ways, privacy is dead. You still have a choice over both your actual behavior and what you share online, both in text and in a photo. With every comment and every share, you are marketing yourself, setting up your reputation, establishing your brand.

Photos can be made public, and people can screenshot almost anything, even Snapchat. If you're looking for a job, future employers will Google you and look at your public photos.

Common Sense Usually Wins

Use your best judgment. If you don't have good judgment, ask a friend, a trusted family member, a professional peer. Online behavior is public behavior. Filter your networks based on intimacy. I think you'll find this to be a natural way to test online friendships.

Disclaimer: Just like in real life, some people can just suck. You can have a friend for 15 years, and they can turn on you. The same can happen online.

CHAPTER 15: GRAMMAR

I've come across many blog posts over the years, whose first paragraph had so severely injured my eyes that I could not continue reading. I've offered to proofread people's posts, and they're offended instead of thanking me for the free help. Guess what? You're standing in the middle of the room with your pants down, and everyone sees it. I'm the one offering a belt. It's your choice whether you view the belt as a tool to inflict punishment or a much-needed support system. Yes, grammar matters.

True, a well-written post about nothing is like a waterless cloud. The need for content does not outweigh the need for its presentation to be, well, presentable. Yes, we all screw up, too. This is not an indictment on your person. I am not condemning you to a life of solitary living on a deserted island with only a dictionary to read. You shouldn't be offended by the post. You should be motivated to improve your writing.

Difficulty Is Not An Acceptable Excuse

Do you want to be taken seriously, or do you want your readers to dismiss your work? Your idea, as good as it may be, is merely the first draft. You still need to proofread.

English is hard. The rules required for grammar, structure, style, spelling, usage, comprehension, and so on, are nuanced and confusing. Even for native speakers! I get that. Heck! Spell check is my friend. Google helps me learn words. It's for that reason that English is one of the few languages with Spelling Bees!

Thankfully, there's plenty of help for all of us with the English language. OWL, the Online Writing Lab at Purdue University, provides free resources for anyone to utilize. The site contains everything you need to know regarding writing in the English language. Less formal resources include blogs, infographics, YouTube tutorials, smartphone apps, and more to help us master English nuances. One of my favorite resources is Copyblogger, where Brian Clark shares the command of the English language and how that relates to online copy. Check out his "15 Grammar Goofs That Make You Look Silly [Infographic][49]" and maybe even bookmark it for reference.

The issue isn't the struggle; it's the results.

Grammar And Proofreading Tips

Formatting can be a distraction to the writing and editing process. Another part of your brain is engaged when you are concerned with the aesthetics of the presentation. This is the case with brochures, websites, and fancy emails. Compose in a plain text file then paste the final version into the appropriate document after proofreading.

Improve your skills. Buy a Secretarial Handbook, follow Grammar Girl, take a class online, or in Adult School. The truth is that there are so many resources available to us (free or low-cost) that there is no excuse to avoid learning and self-improvement. All of these tips aren't required, but they may be helpful.

- If you always struggle with the same error (you're / your), put a sticky note on your computer to remind yourself.

- Avoid contractions. This way, you won't mix up you're and your or its, and it's.

- Print out your draft and read the post backward.

- Read the text out loud. Yep. You sound crazy. This method brings your ears into the work party, and you may hear a mistake your eyes missed. You can combine this step with the first and read the post backward and aloud.

- Get another set of eyes to read your post. This isn't always practical for the person who works at home. Do not choose a nice person. You want the detail-oriented friend who will tell you that you have cilantro stuck in your teeth. This is their role in your life.

- Wait: Copyblogger suggests, "Sit on what you think is your final draft for 24 hours." This is something I need to do more often. Since my drafts wait so long to be posted, it rarely happens.

CHAPTER 16: INTRODUC-TIONS

"Nobody gets anywhere in life without the help of others." ~ John C Maxwell[50]

Meeting New People

Gone are the days when you read every randomly pinned business card on the laundromat's bulletin board while waiting for your clothes to dry. But even that is better than opening up the Yellow Pages (does anyone still have those?) and finding what you need. Your fingers would have to walk miles. Meeting people is always challenging. Sometimes, it is our biggest question. How do you meet a particular person? Find a plumber? Who will you know at the exciting conference next month?

Part of being social is getting to know people. (What a concept, right?) It may just be me, but sometimes I think two people have more in common with each other (than with me). I simply send out a tweet.

> "Hey, @soandso. You should check out @myfriend because you both [insert commonality]"

In social media, introductions are an excellent way to build a following and community. Your people know people you don't know. Introductions can turn into connections. Connections can become trusted, respected, friends, and professional peers. As these relationships develop, those people your people knew and introduced you to...well, they can become clients.

This was the original purpose of #FollowFriday or #FF tweets: to introduce you to people you may not know, but should.

Case(s) In Point

Rhonda Burgin and her husband have a residential design-build contracting business. But she wanted to spice up her SEO. Of course, I sent her to my good friend (who I also met on Twitter), Pam Aungst of Pam Ann Marketing. Burgin Construction, Inc. was Pam's client for years. They got busy and didn't renew. Happy coincidence? Maybe.

I met Asia Bautista of Window Works CA and Motor Works CA through work (she was a window film subcontractor.) She wanted to get more social, so I gave her quite a bit of advice. However, her main issue was time, and she wanted to outsource it. One of my terrific friends, Carol Stephen, whom I met on Twitter, also lives in the Bay Area, so I set the two up. (Notice a pattern in where my good friends come from?)

They've been business associates and friends ever since. Not surprisingly, as connections resemble spider webs more than two-dimensional lines, Asia expressed an interest in improving her search results. Carol introduced her to Pam Ann Marketing.

Of course, I wrote about how I introduced my boss to my newest CRE broker Allen C Buchanan-here. That turned into several referrals. You hear more of his tips on "How to take your relationship offline."

Be A People Curator

Here's the challenge. Think about the people you know, and then think about which contacts you think should know each other. Now: make the introduction. It's not about friend poaching. It's about introductions. Do you know a great restaurant in San Diego? Is your cousin going to vacation there? Introduce them. People will come to value you as a broker of sorts, and maybe, just maybe, they'll return the favor.

CHAPTER 17: GENEROSITY

"It does not do to leave a live dragon out of your calculations if you live near him." J. R. R. Tolkien

Have you encountered a generous person online? They're the ones who make you feel special, though they follow thousands or tens of thousands of people. How do they do it? Often it's more useful to define concepts by their opposites. Being selfish or stingy is regarded as anti-social behavior both online and off. Yet, this creature manifests itself brazenly on social media all of the time. You may haven't intended to hold back but realize you're not getting very much engagement. Is it because you post and go?

If I've said it once, I've said it a hundred times: If you want to have friends, you have to be a friend.

"...if you get on Twitter, and present yourself as a business with a reputation for helping others, guess what, the law of reciprocity is going to come back and help you at some point." Darren Slaughter[51] "Ten Ways Contractors Should Be Using But Aren't."

Twitter

- Did a new account just follow you? Send out a welcome Tweet. Something like: "Hey @soandso - Welcome to Twitter! Nice to see another _____ on the block." I do this a lot with my construction peeps.

- Upon a new follow, finding a recent tweet to favorite or retweet is a great thing.

- An Old School Retweet is a way to expose someone to a different and maybe wider audience.

- Listing followers by category or geography is generous. They can be found among their peers.

- Embed a tweet in your blog, which extends the life of a tweet. Quoting is promoting.

- Are you going to an event? Peruse the Event Hashtag and follow people and respond to tweets.

- Though hosting Twitter chats is Twitter 401, it is an effective way to expose people to a targeted (topic centered) audience.

Pinterest

- Credit people in comments.
- Pin blog posts you read.
- Repin other people's pins.
- Join Group Boards
- Follow new people back.

Facebook Pages

- When a new Facebook Page likes yours, check their page out.
- Like their Facebook Page.
- Comment on one of their posts.
- Share one of their posts.

LinkedIn
- Comment on posts from your peers.
- Endorse people.
- Recommend jobs to people.
- Write genuine recommendations for your peers.

Instagram

- Follow people back.
- Search hashtags and find new people to follow. Comment on a few recent photos (going back too far can be perceived as creepy).
- Comment on their posts and stories.
- Respond to comments on your photos.
- Share their posts through your stories (not regramming which is against the terms of service.)

Blogging
- Embed tweets.
- Subscribe to other people's blogs.
- Credit people who inspired you to write the post (link to their blog).
- Quote people in your blog post -- quoting is promoting.
- Comment on other people's blogs. The more substantive the comment, the more it's appreciated.
- Tweet, Post, Pin, or Share the blog post and tell us why we should read it.
- Interview some of your favorite people that may not have exposure to a broader audience.
- Allow guest posts for those who aren't ready to publish on their own blog (yet).

You should notice a theme: follow, comment, share. This is altruistic behavior. Rinse and Repeat. These tips cross over to any social platform. If I left one-off, apply the concept. I promise that in time you will see the generosity paid back to you.

CHAPTER 18: FOCUS

So you have tons of ideas, and you're scattered here and there, and oh look, a butterfly. We get it. I get it. Heck. I had three personal websites with blogs for this reason. I have finally pared it down to one - bridgetwillard.com. But, even as you look at the micro, you must focus at least on a topic. My blog is about social media, tactics, and strategy, not about photography or business planning.

When it comes to curating an audience around your content, it's helpful if you focus. What is your passion? Focus on that. What is your best source of knowledge? Hone in on it.

Focus On A Series Of Blog Posts

Pick a theme: stick with it for 3-10 posts, more even, to help you stay focused on your content. I started to worry that my social media advice had run its course, quite literally. Then I wrote a post titled *Keys to Being Social: Reciprocation*. The fact that it sounded like a series sort of kicked me in gear. I wrote out some titles, filled out the series, published them as individual blog posts, and eventually assembled for this book. After I heavily edited the *Keys to Being Social Series* for the book format, here we are! (Who am I kidding? I hired Sarah Philips to edit this.)

Want another real example? Check out how many posts Carol Stephen wrote referencing clowns.

Create A Series Of Content For Videos

I was encouraged by a friend to start doing more on my YouTube channel. (Yes, even I need encouragement.) Since something is better than nothing, I impulsively recorded my first #GuruMinute video and tweeted it, without watching it first.

Did I come up with the hashtag right out of the gate? No. Did I have an outline of ideas? Admittedly, no. I thought about the tweets that went back and forth between the two of us, got to work early, and said, "What the heck? I'll do one about how to start a conversation on Twitter! People always ask me that."

The one video gave me an idea for another and the next another idea. The more videos I've done, the more ideas I get. Once I got to three one-minute-or-less videos, I looked to see if the hashtag #GuruMinute was being used. Nope! Winning! I edited the titles of my video and created a playlist. Now, I shoot video spontaneously as the ideas come, and time allows.

Is video a different focus than the blog? No. The tips are still about social media strategy and tactics. It's just another form. I call it the appetizer to the main course (blog).

Tell Your Story

I know I don't have everything pre-planned. I'm not Julia Childs. There aren't measured ingredients on my granite countertops prepared by interns just waiting for me to make magic. I'm just a regular person like you. And I'm just sharing my story through my blog posts and social media content. You can share your story, too.

Do something better than posting platitudes. Anyone can do that. Why does the quote inspire you? How are you applying this to your life?

Does the saying, *If you can dream it, you can do it!* actually help anyone? Maybe. But gentle nudges always help!

Writing Prompts: Just Get Going

I believe anyone can learn to be social, creative, and express themselves. Find your passion, focus on it, and get going. Only you can create your content. What are you waiting for? What could you possibly have to lose?

Here are some writing prompts to jog the creative side of your brain.

Are you a:	You can create:	About:	Such As:	Your Audience:
Homemaker?	Blog Posts Social Media Posts Videos Infographics Photography	Household Management	Cooking Sewing Budgeting	Facebook Page Pinterest Blogging Communities
Wanderlust?	Blog Posts Social Media Posts Videos Infographics Photography	Travel Skills	Best Places to Visit Travel on a Dime Must Have Travel Gear	Twitter Instagram Pinterest
Organizational Enthusiast?	Blog Posts Social Media Posts Videos Infographics Photography	Moving Past the Decluttering	Organizational Tips Favorite File System Small Space Organization	Pinterest Instagram YouTube

CHAPTER 19:
BE FRIENDLY

Sometimes my blog posts end up being confessions of my failures, and this one is no exception. Perhaps epitomes visit me more frequently after a failure.

The Failure

I was invited to the media preview for the Festival of Arts Pageant of the Masters (#FestivalPageant) on June 2, 2014. Though I recognized many people there, I froze. I could not muster up the strength to "say hello to others." A kindly friend came and teased me a bit about hiding and went back to his group. My sister and mom texted me through that event, and I focused on tweeting and enjoying the art.

The Redemption

That weekend, I went to Orange County Word-Camp with friends Carol Stephen and Peter Wool-vett. Being in a group felt much more comfortable to greet others, especially when Peter or Carol did it first. Saying hello to others can be difficult, especially if you're feeling unsure of yourself. But with a little bit of help and prompting from other friends, it's made even more natural. Being a receiver of the greeting helps, too.

While waiting for opening remarks right before Chris Lema's blogging class, we met @Student_OTC. He was a bit surprised that we three had met on Twitter, our second WordCamp that year. We got to learn that he's a web developer somewhat new to WordPress, and it was nice to make him feel welcome.

Bridget Willard
@YouTooCanBeGuru

~ @Student_OTC Seriously, welcome to WordCamp. These people are THE BEST. #WCOC

9:11 AM · Jun 7, 2014 · Twitter Web Client

I looked behind me during those opening remarks and saw Jen Miller, whom I met earlier at Social Media Mastermind OC. Not wanting to interrupt, I sent her a hello tweet. Later in the day, we ended up sitting behind her, and I could both say hello and introduce her to Carol.

Bridget Willard
@YouTooCanBeGuru

Hi @JenBlogs4U #wcoc

8:58 AM · Jun 7, 2014 · Twitter for iPhone

View Tweet activity

1 Like

Carol and I also waved to and met Aaron Hockley, whose blog post "Ultimate Guide: Conference Tips and Hacks[52]" was helpful to read. Carol brought a power strip (aka friend maker) to the conference from that post, and we were glad to use it.

The After Party

Not wanting to be rude, we thought we'd make an appearance at the after-party, mostly since a few people wanted to meet us there. I was stunned to be greeted by none other than Jeffrey Zinn, one of the WCOC organizers. He expressed thankfulness for all of my tweets (I'm obnoxious like that), which made me feel like I belonged. Remarkably, in this geek conference, I was way below my pay grade.

Also, Alex Vasquez greeted me, and I had a friendly yet brief chat. We tweeted @DowntownRob (aka @WebWizards), and he and his son came to chat, and we laughed about a selfie that looked just like Gary Vaynerchuk. I also waved at someone whom I thought had recognized me but didn't. That happened a few times, too. Embarrassing? Yes. What's the worst that could happen? They tweet that some random person waved and said, "Hi?" I doubt it.

Press Wizards WP Dev @PressWizards · Jun 7, 2014
Hope to meet some awesome new peeps at the #wcoc afterparty tonight, who's going?

💬 2   🔁   ♡ 1   ⬆️

Carol Stephen @Carol_Stephen · Jun 7, 2014
@WebWizards Hope to meet awesome new peeps at the #wcoc afterparty tonight, who's going? << Me and @customerspecs + @YouTooCanBeGuru

💬 2   🔁 1   ♡ 2   ⬆️

Press Wizards WP Dev @PressWizards · Jun 7, 2014
@Carol_Stephen @CustomerSpecs @YouTooCanBeGuru Ah nice, let's meet up and say hi. I'll follow from my personal account @DowntownRob as well.

💬 4   🔁   ♡   ⬆️

Bridget Willard @YouTooCanBeGuru · Jun 7, 2014
@WebWizards We're here! Table by the stage.
#wcoc @Carol_Stephen @CustomerSpecs @DowntownRob

💬 1   🔁 1   ♡ 2   ⬆️   ili

The Lunch Line

Do you talk to strangers while waiting in line? I usually don't. On Sunday in the line for the food truck, Verious Smith started chatting with me. We had a great chat about social media strategy and which platforms are better suited for differing industries. And that's not to mention the countless small-talk encounters that never advanced as far as getting their Twitter handle.

The Lesson

So why the WordCamp recap? It's simple. Sometimes we need to be greeted, and sometimes we need to greet others. Depending upon the situation, that changes. The week was up and down. I went from an anxiety attack on Monday to a weekend of full-on fun. That said, the experience has given me more courage to say hello in the future.

We have the power to make people comfortable, and it comes in one word: "Hello." How will you use your power?

CHAPTER 20:
HUMANITY

"The most important thing is for you to be a
human being."
Bridget Willard, Digital Influence Q&A

We are consciously or subconsciously,
both in love with and afraid of technology. Will it someday overtake us?
Has it ruined our relationships? We're the revolu-
tionaries - the defenders of our culture. It's up to
us to retain, protect, and demonstrate our humanity in this digital age. Does modern technology de-
prive us of the natural, spontaneous, if not seren-
dipitous, moments of human connection?

Internet Paper Dolls

When your social posts revolve around one topic, you are two-dimensional, like a paper doll.

As a kid, I had the Holly Hobbie paper doll and I loved it. She had the cutest paper doll clothes. But she was more limited than a Barbie. You couldn't brush or style her hair, only fold over a paper hat. And Holly Hobbie's paper doll definitely couldn't go with you to the beach.

Automating Your Social Experience

I'll admit that social media automation is a debated issue. I'm sure many of my more technical peers will denounce my warning. But I see automation of social media as the Internet Paper Doll. The experience - for both the creator and their audience - is two-dimensional. Pure automation is akin to an RSS feed. That's potentially helpful, but not social. At what point does the time saved by automation make your account less enjoyable to follow? That is an actual risk.

Set it and Forget it

The most significant risk is the set-it-and-forget-it mentality, which is the original allure. It puts you in a position of only responding to mentions (and often not promptly) unless you actively spend time in your lists and/or home feed.

Overexposure

Another risk is overexposure. Automation often includes cross-posting to multiple platforms at the same time. It's easy but not as effective. You run the risk of saturating your market and losing followers on one or more platforms. Who wants to see the same posts on five networks simultan-eously? I don't.

Social Deficit

Another risk is the expenditure of your social capital. If you're automating, you're probably not spending time on the network of choice and sharing other people's content.

Non-Responsive

Automation puts you in a reactionary state, not a responsive state.

> "Automating tweets is like sending a mannequin to a networking event. Stick a post-it note on it, and roll it into multiple events around the world! Think of all the Chamber of Commerce mixers you could cover! Different time zones! Let the relationships windfall begin!!! Booyah!!!" Scott Stratten[53]

Technology Driven Human Connection

Social media isn't a computer doing math problems to make our accounting systems more accurate. Social media isn't a coffee maker that wakes you up with a fresh cup by your bed. The purpose of social media is to give us a platform to meet new people and develop relationships. It's that simple.

Go ahead and schedule your tweets for the day. Install an app to tweet out your old blog posts. Make recipes. Join tribes. That's fine. That technology is only supplemental. You do need to add more of "you" in your stream.

But remember, we connect over commonalities: the minutia, the trivial information about our lives. Dogs, yogurt, sports teams, kids activities, and so on. The content - the connection - is delivered on a new platform but the goal, and end result, can be the same as meeting new neighbors, school parents, married couples. Modern day technology allows us to expand our social circles from the street we live on to the world at large.

The Third Dimension

Small talk makes the world go around. Talk about your pets, vacations, and favorite sports teams. We build our relationships this way every single day around every water cooler on this planet. That said, revealing a little bit of our soul's hopes, dreams, ambitions, or fears is how we deepen these relationships. Yes, this requires some vulnerability on your part, but vulnerability is a powerful force. Your vulnerability in your online social encounters brings that third dimension to the table.

CHAPTER 21:
BE PRESENT

Are we in a race to be noticed? Do we take time to enjoy the moment? During a Women In Business Today interview, Kittie Walker of Avidmode brought up an interesting point. "Networking events aren't speed dating." She makes an excellent point about having deep, meaningful conversations.

Of course, I had to apply that to social media. I noticed a feeling that I've been behind on Facebook. I feel pressure to like and comment, and I find myself scrolling - looking for things to like. So I like, and like, and like. Whew. I'm caught up. But what have I accomplished?

Distracted Listening

I always go to my lists on Facebook first, primarily to notice posts from my family members. That said, there's a feeling that I'm missing something. It dawned on me. I've become that jerk looking around the room for someone else to talk to while I'm currently in the middle of a conversation. I don't want to be that person. I didn't start as that person.

If there's someone I'm curious about, I can always look up their name and see what posts I've missed. The last week or so, I've just trusted Facebook to show me what they think I should see.

It's not always easy to comment. Quite frankly, content creators and curators like myself are always pushing our audience to read something then discuss. Still, Kitty's thought is in my head. Isn't it better for me to engage with this one person right now than to scroll-like-scroll-like? And, if Person X always posts content you or I don't like on Facebook, then perhaps it is time to question the connection. Am I that busy? Or am I just too lazy to read that article or watch that video? These are real questions I have to ask myself. Am I present or just online?

CHAPTER 22: LOYALTY

As I reflect on my social media philosophy, another one that must also be spoken for is loyalty.

Loyalty is the superglue of relationships. It's what keeps the bonds originally formed intact. It requires maintenance and upkeep, especially if conflict arises. Loyalty is a two-way street; feelings of betrayal come when the expectation of loyalty is violated. Loyalty is shown when it is least expected but most needed. Loyalty, in times of trouble, solidifies a relationship.

It comes from the actual business owners I've come to know, like, and trust. From relationships that I've built meeting people online, at conferences, and at work. It comes from experiencing the intrinsic value of loyalty (and sometimes there are perks to follow.)

Loyalty, I believe, is the heart of the shop local movement.

Intrinsic Value Of Loyalty

I think about the deli I loved that recently moved to Portland. Valuing social media, I found The Real Deli because of Twitter and we formed a relationship afterward based on quality product and customer experience. The loyalty between us both came about from mutual respect, and now I consider them friends.

While they were here, I couldn't eat at just any sandwich shop. They were my friends. Though my favorite deli was more expensive than Subway, the few extra bucks I spent were more valuable to me than Subway prices. I felt good supporting a local business that had won my heart, and in return I gained new relationships.

It was the best turkey sandwich I ever had. And I guess it was the best turkey sandwich a lot of people loved because the deli was popular enough to be sold. My new friends left to find culinary adventures in Portland. I was excited to tell all of my Portland friends to like their new Facebook Page.

Physical Perks Of Loyalty

Loyalty doesn't "just" feel good, it can sometimes come with some fun perks! Being friendly, delivering a product, and "loyalty" rewards in the form of special events passes, free coffee drinks, or free tiramisu desserts after dine-in experiences, are endless, but there's more!

- I have enjoyed the beautiful hor's d' oeuvre plates prepared by a professional chef just because I had a Twitter conversation with his wife.
- Churro love, delivered to me from my favorite Mexican eatery after they noticed I left a review of their restaurant on Facebook.
- Receiving surprise books in the mail from new friends who enjoyed my new twitter chat.
- A couple of Twitter friends sent me an edible arrangement to cheer me up, simply because they knew I needed the encouragement right at that very moment.
- My favorite florist, who supported me during two recent hard funerals, allowed me to use their shop as a backdrop - because they care.
- Getting thank-you notes and Starbucks cards to those who I helped finish a project on time.
- Getting an unexpected private message thanking me for my help.
- Colluding with a friend to buy a mutual friend a plane ticket after her mother's untimely

death.

- An online friend posted a photo of sunflowers on my Facebook wall, just to brighten my day.
- Readers who value my blog content have linked their blog to mine, inadvertently bringing me a new client!
- Being added to a "Super Fan," "ThankYou," or "Appreciation" list on Twitter, and seeing my content being shared across different channels.

All of these are the perks of loyalty - the reciprocation given...just because.

Loyal Reciprocation

Loyalty is not about just being nice to get free stuff. It's about building relationships online the same way we would build relationships offline.

One week I tweeted that the outsole on one of my brand new ZipZ shoes started to break. I was hoping for some general advice on proper glue for shoes. The [brand name shoe] business read my tweet, looked up my customer account information, and emailed me -that same day - to let me know a new pair of shoes was in the mail. They were grateful for my business, valued me as a customer, and understood how inconvenient this was for me.

I didn't slam them. I pointed out an issue. I stayed loyal to the company. They reciprocated in-kind.

Loyalty Vs. Convenience

Customers come from relationships, but they stay because of loyalty. Companies that show commitment to consumers will receive their customer's loyalty. That's not to confuse loyalty with convenience. Convenience can't be taken for granted, mind you. It is a powerful extension of reach - of good customer service to the customer.

It's easy to confuse the two, so here's a great example. I'm thankful for Starbucks and their 12thstar free latte. I stay with them because it's convenient (good app, lots of stores, consistent quality), not because I'm necessarily loyal to their brand. If the coffee place I love was closer to my house, had an app with a rewards program, or even an in-house rewards program, and a variety of locations, I might leave Starbucks forever. I'm not loyal to Starbucks; I'm loyal to the *CONVENIENCE* of Starbucks.

CHAPTER 23:
RESPOND

Disclaimer: This bit may be a bit controversial.
If you decide to burn my effigy, do it responsibly
with a fire department truck on
standby like Mythbusters.

Part of being a social person on social media is responding. [Crowd gasps, gathers stones.] I know, I know, this is crazy talk. But if social media is about building relationships, you MUST respond to the conversation happening right in front of you. (Otherwise you're just a creepy lurker!) But there is a right way and a lot of wrong ways to participate in responding to social media conversations. Let's break it down.

First, Manners Matter

> *"What you do not want done to yourself, do not do to others."* Confucius[54]

I believe in responding with my whole heart. It ties into the Golden Rule (aka basic manners). When I'm teaching this, I usually ask, "Would you do [insert online behavior here] in real life?" If no, then don't do it online. If yes..well...then a refresher in universally accepted manners is in store for you!

Manners Are Respect

"Good manners are not about doing everything perfectly right, they are about being thoughtful and using common sense, about choosing civility over rudeness."
Jill Evans Kryston[55]

We often say social media is about building relationships. How is that done? It's undoubtedly not Sea Monkeys. (Those instant aquariums of brine shrimp that you just add water to.) It doesn't mean that you have to go on vacation with your newest follower either. People seem to respond to me with extremes, so I wanted to clear that up. But we can break it down to a demonstration of mutual respect. Ignoring someone does not show respect.

Manners Take Time

"You had to spend time with [brands] to get to know them as people." Ted Rubin[56]

People often say that's not really scalable. I think this is an excuse. When I see responses from Ted Rubin or Gary Vaynerchuk then you definitely have the time. Do you have 250,000 followers or over a million? Most likely, the people in my audience have under 5,000.

Manners And Automation

We've covered this before: the danger in over-automating via the "set it and forget it" mentality. You've made a recipe or installed a plugin that automatically tweets/posts for you. However, if you aren't paying attention and minding your audience, a few things may happen.

For example, let's say your blog is auto-posting new blog posts to your Facebook Page, but you fail to check your notifications and rarely engage with your audience. You're trying to grow a healthy Facebook Page, but you're shooting yourself in the foot. Probable outcomes for your Facebook Page growth will be:

 A. People comment, you don't respond.
   a. First, your automated post on Facebook will not be served to very many people.
   b. Second, you've wasted their time by ignoring their comments - which comes across as rude.
 B. People stop commenting. Most reasonable people will stop commenting when they're ignored. I know how I feel when I'm ignored, I feel unvalued and I stop engaging with the brand.
   a. First, your automated post on Facebook will no longer be served

across your network.

b. Second, you will have trouble gaining new Facebook Page Likes, which means your Facebook Page is not growing.

C. Third, people who want the attention of your network, your community, will comment regardless if you do.

a. First, your Facebook Page can be marked as spam and thrown into Facebook Jail.

b. Second, you've lost control over your Facebook Community and your brand. The third group of people is whom you end up having.

This is the WORST possible outcome for your Facebook Page. You will have to work pretty hard to recover this.

Paying attention to your audience isn't just being polite and mannerly. You have a responsibility to nurture, grow, and engage with your audience. Otherwise, what is the point?

Responses Require Manners

What defines social is behavior, not an account on a "social platform." We talked about engagement in a recent #BufferChat, and I liked this answer from Christin Kardos:

> **Christin Kardos** ⭐ **#CMGR, backseat Harley rider** ⭐
> @ChristinKardos
>
> **A2) Engagement is 2** way communication. TWO **WAY.**
> **Listening is key to this,** following up is mission crit**ical.**
> #BufferChat
>
> 9:14 AM · Nov 12, 2014 · Nurph

The minimal response is a plus, like, favorite, or heart. I believe those verbs cover the basis of social platforms. It's the equivalent of a wink or a wave across a crowded room. No other response is warranted. It could also mean, "I read your post." This is the lowest level commitment of what I would consider a legitimate response. This behavior takes less than ten seconds.

A more generous response, especially if User X writes a well-thought-out comment or sends a tweet, responds in kind. Humans are wired to mirror responses. I smile, you smile; I frown, you frown. This experience can be translated into the digital space.

I generally thank people for their time. "Thank you for taking the time to read and comment; I appreciate it."

Additionally, I respond to the content in their comment by expanding on my thoughts. "I use favorites to bookmark my tweets to read later."

It does take time, effort, and energy. But I believe if you treat your audience with respect, that respect will be returned to you with loyalty.

CHAPTER 24: DISCRETION

Our society worships youth. Does it go back to the '60s or Ponce de León's quest for the Fountain of Youth? Either way, the effect is the same. New technology breeds the expectation that youth, who have grown up with it, are the most qualified. But I think any generation lacks something their senior generations have: discretion.

Sure, they may be able to play Nintendo from the womb, but it's not enough. The young of today may have left Facebook for Snapchat. They may know how to buy songs online. But does this mean they have the advantage over Gen X or even Baby Boomers? I say no.

Listen up, Gen Y, Millennials, and anyone else born after 1990. You have to develop a sense of discretion.

Discretion

Merriam-Webster defines discretion as: "the right to choose what should be done in a particular situation: the quality of being careful about what you do and say so that people will not be embarrassed or offended: the quality of being discreet."

And, pray tell, how does one get this quality? More often than not, by experience. The older we get, the more we're able to learn by other people's mistakes. The "folly of youth," as they say, is to make many mistakes.

Discretion is also a function of judgment and inhibition. The human brain hasn't fully developed until the age of 25.

> *"Neuroscience has shown that a young person's cognitive development continues into this later stage and that their emotional maturity, self-image, and judgment will be affected until the prefrontal cortex of the brain has fully developed." Lucy Wallis[57]*

Foolishness

I think we call much behavior stupid when foolish is the right word. The problem isn't a lack of learning or intelligence, the problem is a lack of discernment. Two news stories caught my eye today that back up my claim that "the youth" shouldn't be automatically viewed as the most qualified. Exhibit A is a story of a teenager's R-rated tweet about her job before she even starts. Exhibit B is a story of a teenage murderer taking a selfie on Snapchat with his victim.

The moral of the story is that nothing is private on the internet. Screenshots give extra life to online photos, tweets, and posts, even those that "disappear." Think of these examples before you hire your niece to do your social media. The young may have technical advantages, but character develops with age, often through hard lessons. Do you want a 16 year old cutting her teeth on your brand's channel?

That's not to say all young people have little to offer in the way of wisdom, discernment, and maturity. It is just to say, you know, use your own wisdom, discernment, and maturity when it comes to managing your social media content and with whom you allow access to your accounts.

CHAPTER 24: VOICE

You're just tweeting, why do you need a voice? By no means is this key one of the first you'll gain mastery of in your social media keychain. Voice is something that develops over time. This week at #BufferChat[58], we talked about finding your voice. That can be a tricky thing. It requires some introspection. When asked, can you answer?[59]

Buffer ✓
@buffer

Q3: What advice would you give to those working on finding their **"voice?"** #bufferchat

9:21 AM · Mar 25, 2015 · Buffer

My Voice

Though I've been on Twitter since 2007, it took me a while to find my voice. Through questions in tweets, text messages, or emails, I realized I needed this forum-- Twitter -- this place to find myself. I needed a place to give my advice and tips, not just for the person asking but also for anyone else. Many small businesses do their own social media. Through my blog, tweets, and videos, I help small businesses using humor and analogies. Yes, I will make a fool of myself for your benefit.

How did that happen? It didn't happen overnight.

I appreciate humor. I was a teacher. I've been a secretary for over twenty years. Now I'm a self-taught social media manager. Did my previous experiences suddenly disappear? No. They make me who I am. This is me after four years of tweeting on this account alone. Finding Your

Your Voice

Don't overwhelm yourself. Think of three things that interest you. Grab a pen and a pencil. Without overthinking, list your primary purpose. Now choose two sides (kind of like a good dinner).

1. Primary Passion: Social Media
   a. Side Passion A: Dogs
   b. Side Passion B: Photography

Now, start creating content about dogs and photography. Start finding other communities online about dogs and photography. Consider what you read; consider how you respond. Try it out. See if these side passions allow you to really communicate in an authentic way online. Are you making connections? Does it feel natural? Then you can analyze the results to see what's working and what isn't.

Having more dimensions to your online presence is one way to be authentic. Figuring out the right combination of topics for you is how you find your voice. So just keep your primary/secondary passion lists growing and eventually you will find your groove - your voice.

It Takes Time

The more you write, speak, sing, or dance, the closer you are to finding your personality. The more experience you have, the more likely you'll fall into your voice. It's the same in social media. Some people say you should know your audience. I say when you find your voice, your audience finds you.

I recently watched "The Improv: 50 Years Behind The Brick Wall," a documentary about The Improv. It affected generations of comedians. They all said how The Improv facilitated their voice-finding process. Jimmy Fallon, in this clip, recounts how he once shaved on stage. It didn't work.

CHAPTER 25: HOSPITALITY

There is nothing worse than feeling unwelcome. We've all been to those parties. Either the host reluctantly agreed to throw the party, or you were one of those hopes-she-says-no invites. But part of being hospitable is merely being a warm person. It starts with a smile and a greeting. So how do we do this digitally?

Intrinsic Value Of Hospitality

Basically, it's not about what you get out of it - it's what you give others.

Have you ever read a blog and wrote a comment where the author never replied? How about a Tweet or a comment on Facebook? These are the kinds of things that make people feel unwelcome. I mentioned this in the section on Manners. Maybe Hospitality is a part of Manners that should be observed and nurtured and developed and strengthened as we progress into our new modern communication methods and habits.

People often say they don't have time. Maybe they don't. But if you care about people, you'll find the time. There are people like Gary Vaynerchuk and Ted Rubin, who manage their accounts and take the time to respond to people organically. Guess what happens? People feel welcome in their community. They feel heard. They feel like they have value. That's hospitality.

Maybe you're that grumpy rich uncle whose behavior is tolerated in hopes that blessings will trickle down. There are always social celebrities that we give a pass. If that's you, you can stop reading now.

Inhospitable Communities

Do you make people feel valuable, wanted, and appreciated? Even if your website is beautiful, your Pinterest Boards are pleasing to the eye, and your Facebook Cover Photo is at the current dimensions, your community can still be inhospitable. It's like going to a well-decorated party where you still feel uncomfortable. Sure, people can bring their issues with them. But we are the ones who set the tone on all of our platforms.

If your community is inhospitable, it's because you've allowed it to become such. You've created an inclusive community who lacks tolerance, deference, and maturity. The culture that permeates across your social communities is your responsibility. Don't dismiss that responsibility just because you're "too busy." If you're too busy for social media, maybe you should reconsider your objectives regarding the use of social channels.

Be More Hospitable

Below are some ways you can work on your hospitality skills. The more you practice, the better
you will get - and soon you'll be a hospitality guru.

Website & Blog:
- Navigation should be easy for the general public.
- Make it easy for people to read about you.
- Ask questions in your posts.
- Make sure it's easy to comment (without a bunch of hoops).
- Make social buttons easy to find.
- Respond to comments.
- Check out their blog (bonus).

Twitter:
- Follow back.
- Don't use things like TrueTwit Validation.
- List (bonus) and engage.
- Respond to tweets.
- Thank people for their retweets (bonus).
- Avatar looks like us. (I know mine is a cartoon, but I have two Twitter accounts, so one is a photo, and the other is a cartoon.)
- Some tweets are conversational (not just all links).

Facebook:

- Post content helpful to your audience.
- Like their comments, this is an acknowledgment.
- Respond to their comments.
- Like other Facebook Pages.
- Interact on other Pages as your Page.
- Like Pages from your account (bonus) and check the Pages feed regularly.

Instagram:

- Ask a question in your post.
- Respond to comments.
- Check out the feed of frequent commenters and comment on their photos.
- Follow other Instagrammers.
- Use community hashtags (find and be found).

Do you notice a trend? Respond. Engage. The same kind of thing goes for Pinterest, Periscope, and whatever new-fangled social media platform comes out next (Ello, Tsu).

CHAPTER 26: LISTENING

As I'm writing this, I'm streaming Pandora in the background, but I'm not listening to the songs. I hear the music, but I'm not paying attention - I'm not listening. Do you feel that people listen when you speak? Not just hear you even, but really, truly listen? People are talking every day on social media. The scale at which information is coming to us can be overwhelming.

"Every second, on average, around 6,000 tweets are tweeted on Twitter." Internet Live Stats[60]

Six thousand tweets per second. Mind you, quite a bit of those are news or content marketing. But think about it - what if only 1% of those tweets were from people just wanting to be heard?

That equates to 60 people a second. If I could insert code that would make this posting pause for 60 seconds, 3,600 tweets would have been sent.

Listening Isn't Hearing

Though listening starts with hearing, it isn't just hearing. Some argue that hearing begins with attention. Attention starts with intent. Therefore, listening begins with intention. When learning a new subject, you muster all of your concentration powers just to absorb and retain. Do we do that in conversation? When you're at lunch with your friend, do you listen to what he or she is saying? Or are you distracted by the waiter, the menu, the noise...or even your phone?

People are telling you all about themselves. It's what they say and what they don't say. It's their body language. Are they facing you? Are they making eye contact? Do they pause and choose their words carefully or just say what comes to mind?

Listening is a prerequisite to connection. You will never feel connected to someone who doesn't listen. And vice versa. Listening is a valuable skill to invest in, in both the physical and digital realm. Be interested in other people and what they have to say.

Two Sides To Listening

When I used to teach Sunday School, I would tell the kids to listen when I wanted to make a point. They'd say, "I hear you, Miss Bridget." But hearing is not listening. Listening isn't waiting for when our name - or brand - is mentioned.

"So, enough about me...but what do YOU think of me?"

We laugh at that joke, but how often is it true? How many people drive you crazy because it's a two-hour monologue every time you go to lunch? If you genuinely care about people, you will care about what they have to say. There are two sides to listening.

You should want to listen to your friend. Of course, you want a friend who listens to you. In our personal, professional, and digital lives, the people who listen are the people who are trusted. They're well-liked. They're successful.

Commit To Listening

Listening requires the listener to be patient and quiet. Both are hard by themselves. Together, to be a quiet, patient listener, it takes determination and commitment.

> "Although listening might sound more difficult than talking, all it requires is that you be fully present." Carol Stephen[61]

To be a good listener, regardless of the situation, you have to set aside your agenda. I've learned this repeatedly in all kinds of situations: one-on-one conversations, business meetings, Bible studies, etc. Yet, I must confess that I fail more often than I'd like. I forget to stop talking. I forget to stop interrupting. I fail to say something I should. I fail to look at them in the face and say, "You are worthy of love. You are valuable."

Digital Listening

So how do you do this online? Easy! Sit on your hands. Just kidding. Well, not really. When you get online to peruse social media, do it with the intent to pay attention to what you are reading and be prepared to offer a response that brings the other readers value.

First, my favorite tool to help me navigate all the noise on Twitter, and be ready to listen to my audience is the use of Twitter Lists. Using curated Twitter lists, I can quickly dive into whichever audience base I want to spend time with, read tweets, and respond when appropriate. This is the best tool for listening digitally. It's that simple.

Second, spend more time reading than replying. Find out who your customers are. Find your friends. Spend time reading your friends' posts on Facebook, instead of your own. Read what they say. Spend time reading someone else's blog, not just refreshing your own Google Analytics. Many days I spend 15-20 minutes just reading tweets on my lists. Why not respond, you ask? It has to do with situational awareness.

Situational Awareness

Have you ever been in a conversation, and then another person walks into the room and just starts talking? It distracts and can be considered obnoxious or rude. Twitter often has conversational tweets. Although Twitter is the most forgiving about "jumping in a conversation," you need context to bring value to the conversation. You only get context if you gain some situational awareness.

I rarely jump in on actual conversations. Instead, I'll reply to a tweet that is directed to the general public. If someone says they're bummed out their computer broke, I'll answer "bummer." If someone is excited to launch a new website, I'll say, "congratulations." Situational awareness is critical, both in-person and online.

Mirroring

You need situational awareness to mirror emotions. We are hard-wired in our brains to reflect emotions. This is why babies smile at us when we smile at them. If someone laughs, laugh with them. When they cry, cry with them. Be empathetic. This is our humanity. This is how we are approachable, authentic, relatable, and likable. We all want to be liked. It all comes down to this: Invest in people, and they'll invest in you.

CHAPTER 27: DIVERSITY

When diversity is discussed, we generally think of it in terms of gender or race. But there is so much more to the value of diversity within our social circles and workplaces. It's great to be with people we like or that like us, but is it the best thing for us? When I have conversations with people about following others, especially within the context of Twitter, one word inevitably pops up: relevant.

"Who's relevant to me?" "I only follow people who are relevant?" So, I'll freely admit that this phrase comes off as short-sighted at best and elitist at worst. So, you want 10,000 followers from whichever backgrounds serve your purpose, but you only want to follow 37? Okay. Whatever.

Relevance is a subjective and self-centered metric.

There's no other way to describe it. Well, Gary Vaynerchuk has a few choice words about this subject, but it's Rated R for Language.

Diversity Matters

"A growing body of research shows that diver-sity—in gender, thinking styles, and intro- and extroversion—is needed for teams to be their most productive." Drake Baer [62]

I understand the need and impulse to create and protect company culture. It's great when you all like doing the same thing and show up for morn-ing yoga sessions. But company culture is more than shared hobbies and shared interests. This is also true of your social media circles. If you only ever listen to people who think exactly how you do, how will you change, grow, or improve?

"By focusing on different skills, we support and balance our partner, instead of competing at the same tasks. Our partnerships promote a diver-sity of thinking, perspective, and knowledge." Stefan Klocek, Cooper[63]

Listen To Outsiders

I recently attended a book signing and talk by Simon Sinek. I saw the event on LinkedIn and asked Jen Miller of NeedSomeoneToBlog.com if she was free. It was close (LA) and $40. There was no reason not to go.

Afterward, we felt so inspired! I had a second wind kick in with my writing for work. Jen called me and said, "we need to go to more of these." His third book <u>Together is Better</u>, follows the theme of his first two: we're social animals, and we need each other.

So, why did I go see Simon Sinek? It has nothing to do with social media. Or does it? If my frame of reference for listening and learning was only focused on social media, I would lose out on a lot. If I were only following people I deemed "relevant," would Simon Sinek make the cut? And what kind of a world would that leave me in? I think this is what it means to live in a silo.

Bridget Willard
@YouTooCanBeGuru

"I'm curious about the world. I'm lucky I still have ideas."
@simonsinek

8:29 AM · Sep 21, 2016 · Twitter for iPhone

The Danger Of a Thought Rut

Jason Knill used to say to me, "Be curious." And that is the key to learning. If you were not curious, you would never ask, "what if?" You would never dream, innovate, create.

If there were no reason to be curious, I'd only listen to the five thought leaders within my industry (WordPress, tech, construction, social media, etc.) That only leads to what I call a thought rut. Many people call it an echo chamber. The point is that it's the same ideas repackaged over and over and over. You're in a rut.

Do we want to regurgitate the ideas someone else is saying over and over and over? Do we only speak jargon without ever understanding its true meaning? Do we take the time to follow the logical conclusion of the presumptions we build within our businesses? In his TED Talk about where ideas come from, Steven Johnson talks about the English coffee house and the birth of the enlightenment.

"But the other thing that makes the coffeehouse important is the architecture of the space. It was a space where people would get together from different backgrounds, different fields of expertise, and share. It was a space, as Matt Ridley

talked about, where ideas could have sex. This was their marital bed, in a sense --ideas would get together there. And an astonishing number of innovations from this period have a coffee-house somewhere in their story." Steven Johnson[64]

Our coffee house can be a co-working space, a meetup, or even Twitter. We should listen to people's ideas, think about them, and consider them for their own sake -- regardless if we believe they are relevant to us. But when we deeply think about other ideas, we allow them to affect us. We allow cross-pollination. I think it's dangerous to only listen to people you agree with -- politically, socially, and creatively. As he said in the video noted above, "Chance favors the connected mind." Steven Johnson

Diversity And Collaboration

I have friends from all walks of life. Long ago, I decided that I would focus on the things we have in common and not argue about the things we disagree about. But still, if you're closed to ideas, you're closed to relationships. Next time you feel like you're in a mental rut, consume. You cannot create without consuming. But consume from something different: read nonfiction, watch a documentary, listen to a comedy podcast, etc. Allow your mind to think about other things, and you will always be ready for serendipity.

CHAPTER 28:
INFLUENCE

"When we communicate, we are influencing, and we are being influenced." Dan Norris[65]

Influence is more than influencer marketing or content marketing. In social media, you can use your influence for so much more. What does that even mean? Is it changing the behavior of people who look up to you? Or is it something more substantive? It comes down to how you communicate. And that fits right into social media. After all, the purpose of social media is communication.

Influence And Change

Influence is "...the power to change or affect someone or something: the power to cause changes without directly forcing them to happen" Merriam-Webster[66]

The problem with influence is that we forget the part after the word power. And maybe, just maybe, influence is more like being a thought leader. And if that's true, how does one become a Thought Leader? Simultaneously, someone who talks about a subject that resonates in your being is a thought leader.

Influential Reach

> *"On average, we live for 78.3 years. Most of us remember people we meet after age 5. Assume we interact with three new people daily in cities, 365 days in a year plus leap year days is 365.24. In total it will be (78.3 – 5) x 3 x 365.24 = 80,000 people. Is it a lot?"* Anna Vital[67]

According to their infographic, you can make an impact on between 14-150 people. That's a lot of people. That's a lot of influence. So, the truth is that everyone influences someone.

Seriously, how many people can we affect?

Five? Twelve? How many people do we meet?

Influence And Content Marketing

Any content marketer worth her salt will be able to persuade in her writing. A public speaker will persuade in his speech. The emails hitting your phone are meant to provoke you to act. Whether it is educational or offers a promotion, all content marketing is intended to persuade and, therefore, influence your behavior. Namely, content marketing's job is to get you to click. Buy now. Sign up. Don't miss out. So don't forget to include a call to action in your copy. I mean, as a content marketer, I'd be a liar if I didn't say I wanted to influence others. Show me that click rate again, yo.

Influencer Marketing

"In the context of Influencer Marketing, influence is less about argument and coercion to a particular point of view and more about loose interactions between various parties in a community. Influence is often equated to advocacy, but may also be negative, and is thus related to concepts of promoters and detractors." Wikipedia[68]

Influencer marketing remains a strong marketing game. One person with substantial social clout could make or break your new apparel line. This type of marketing stems from celebrity endorsements.

Employing the science of influence and persuasion, including the principles from Influence At Work: "reciprocity, scarcity, authority, consistency, and liking," will help your effort to influence. These tactics can help us with our marketing efforts, increase sales, and affect affinity. Any power can be used for less-than-altruistic purposes, but most of these behaviors are just good manners.

Influence Vs. Encouragement

Influence is the ability to affect someone for your

benefit. We can use our words to give courage (encourage) or take it away (discourage).

Encouragement is "something that makes someone more determined, hopeful, or confident" Merriam-Webster[69]

Unfortunately, there have been many discouraging moments in my life. Words rang in my ears, rattled in my brain, and paralyzed me -- for years.

> "You're never going to be special
> enough for that stage."

> "You're never going to play guitar."

> "You're not a writer."

Do we want to do that, just to make ourselves feel better? I have a choice, and you have a choice: we can listen to people. We can know them and guide their next steps. We can be a mentor. We can use our influence to make them bigger, stronger, more confident. That's the kind of influence that matters -- and it cannot be measured or be included in KPI reporting.

Influence Vs. Legacy

I choose legacy - the kind of legacy that isn't about me. I want to know that people's lives were changed; to see that previously timid person stand with chest lifted, shoulders down and back, chin up, face forward, hands-on hip. I want to see them thrive. I want to watch them achieve their goals. I want people to look back and say that I helped them believe in themselves. That's the legacy I want. What about you?

CHAPTER 29: VULNERABILITY

"The thing that underpinned this was excruciating vulnerability. This idea of, in order for connection to happen, we have to allow ourselves to be seen, really seen." Brené Brown[70]

Being open with people permits them to be open with you. But how transparent should you be? How much should you tell? What does vulnerability have to do with social media? My friend Carol recently said, "I liked what you said about not wanting things to be weird with people not knowing where you were when you next met them."

Vulnerability

Vulnerability is defined as being "susceptible to emotional injury, especially in being easily hurt:" The Free Dictionary[71]

How does vulnerability affect social media? It's about connection. The more connections you have, the more influence you have. As scary as it is, vulnerability is vital. I've been thinking about it for years -- but Brené Brown's famous TED Talk helped keep my thoughts alive.

I asked my friend, "Would you agree that being open gives people permission to be open with you?" She answered, "Most definitely. It's not easy to show vulnerability, though, with practice, vulnerability puts others more at ease." Carin Arrigo[72]

She's right. Think of the people you feel most safe around. Are they the people who are open to you?

Vulnerability And Connection

In her TED Talk, Brené Brown recounts how studying vulnerability caused her to have a breakdown of her own. She told her therapist:

> *"And I know that vulnerability is the core of shame and fear and our struggle for worthiness, but it appears that it's also the birthplace of joy, of creativity, of belonging, of love."* Brené Brown[73]

And who doesn't want joy? Who doesn't want to feel creative? Who doesn't wish to belong and love? I found this out in my bout of songwriting. My album[74]'s producer, Chris Falson[75], used to say that a songwriting partnership was a lot like a marriage. At first, it seems like a ridiculous analogy. But when I thought about it further, it made sense. To be creative with another person, you have to trust them. You have to trust that person deeply. Your ideas, your creativity, come from your soul. Creativity is closely tied to our identity. If you've ever brainstormed with someone who made you feel stupid for "throwing an idea out there," you know how unsafe it can feel to be vulnerable.

Social media thrives off of connection. Maybe you don't need it. If your only goal is to sell tchotchkes, as my friend Steve Zehngut says, then build an e-commerce site and be done with it. If loyalty and reciprocation are essential to you, and influence is something you want, you need connection. The unavoidable truth is that we will never experience deep and lasting relationships without vulnerability.

"In a world where people compare their behind-the-scenes with others' highlight reels, we can surprise ourselves, and put others at ease, by sharing our full humanity." Michael Simmons, Harvard Business Review[76]

Vulnerability And Discernment

And so I return to the question I asked Carin. "Would you agree that being open gives people permission to be open with you?" And I say, to that, "absolutely." That said, and I have told friends and colleagues this, share what you feel comfortable sharing. But I would still advise that you share something personal. Whatever that thing is -- a hobby, perhaps -- that will allow someone to start a dialog with you. Share that.

Vulnerability And Shame

Keeping secrets means internalizing stress. And secrets come from shame or the fear of it. Many years ago at a women's retreat, Lauren Kitchens -- a famous radio personality -- told us to make friends and acquaintances. Open ourselves up to people. But she put her arms in front of her in a circle, miming holding a bucket and said, "Not everyone gets to be in my bucket." And she's right. A few friends should be close to you. A few people that you can trust are suitable for these deep things. But at the same time, being open relieves stress.

> "When I finally got up the courage to start telling the truth, I could feel a weight lift off my shoulders. I had no idea how much stress I had been causing myself. To my huge surprise, instead of shunning me, people treated me with more respect and confided in me with their challenges to my huge surprise. I wondered how I had been so wrong in judging other people's reactions." Michael Simmons[77]

Less stress, more respect, and possibly feeling more connected to this world impacts your work performance. If you're in a management position, this could quite literally change your bottom line.

> "You see, if the conditions are wrong, we are
> forced to expend our own time and energy to pro-
> tect ourselves from each other, which inherently
> weakens the organization. When we feel safe in-
> side the organization, we will naturally combine
> our talents and strengths and work tirelessly to
> face the dangers outside and seize the opportun-
> ities." Simon Sinek[78]

Vulnerability And Boundaries

No one wants to be real. But you need to be real -- with somebody. Even in counseling or mentorship, you have to open up or you'll never have the healing and insight. During the business track at WordCamp Orange County, Tami Heaton discussed finding out she had boundary issues.

> *"Nobody likes to plunge into the depths of their soul to see what's dysfunctional."* Tami Heaton[79]

My friend Adam Fout, whom I met on Twitter, by the way, is vulnerable. His writing is real. It's raw. It speaks to me. And guess what? I feel more connected to him. Not in a weird stalker way, but in an I-trust-you way. Here's a sample about perfectionism and creativity that he wrote. (He's right, too. Perfectionism is crippling.)

> *"Perfectionism kills what could be amazing creations while they're still in the cradle. Perfectionism also turns ideas that should have died long ago into shambling zombies. These zombies keep me from moving on to something fresh. It also does this lovely thing where it fills me with guilt and shame when I publish something that doesn't meet its exacting standards. And never,*

not once, has perfectionism actually given me a perfect product. It's a character defect, and the more time I spend trying to kill it, the better of a creator I become (I think).

Because when the lie that nothing I create is good enough goes away, I might actually create something decent." Adam Fout[80]

Vulnerability Is Terrifying

I suffered a great loss when my husband of 23 years died of complications from Kidney Disease. During his hospitalizations, I had always been open about it: to let his friends and family know what was going on, to receive prayer, to be real. And because I had opened myself up on Facebook during his last hospitalization, about a dozen of my friends knew when he died.

I came home from the hospital, not knowing, but thinking, I would not even have enough money for his cremation. Little did I know that this tribe of mine spent six hours -- during the night while I wept and finally fell asleep -- to set up willard-fund.org. When I woke up, I had enough funds to cover the cremation and funeral costs.

As I grieved this incredible loss, I spent time decompressing and putting my thoughts down -- on Facebook -- for my friends to read and pray for me. I knew that if I didn't speak of his death -- my grief -- that people would feel awkward around me the next time we ran into each other. Should they talk about Mercier? Should they ask how I'm doing? And if I self-isolated, that would make my feelings of grief and loneliness worse.

Carol suggested that I write a post called "Social Media Spotlight: Being Open with People." As I'm sitting down and looking deep within my drafts

folder, I thought this topic is really about the ter-
rifying emotional state of vulnerability.

Value Of Vulnerability

All of these pieces fit together in a beautiful mess. We are all trying. We get up and go to work and make our business the best it can be. There is no business Nirvana. We see viral posts online and wonder why we can't attain that perfection. But it isn't real. It's a mirage.

"How much would it cost to get 10,000 followers," I was asked on a consulting call.

"Five years." I replied. Why? You can't buy loyalty. And loyalty is the byproduct of vulnerability.

Vulnerability is the portal by which social media stops being virtual. There are real people on the other side of those screens. They have hopes and dreams and fears and desires. They have frustrations. You have solutions. The value of vulnerability is the connections we make that last longer than any financial transaction. It's the tribe of people we build around us.

People want to be part of your story and the only way is to let them in. Those true connections will be your referral network. They will offer the most sincere praise that would make Yelp blush. They will champion for you when you have those days -- the days we all have -- when we think we should just join the Peace Corps and be done with this digital life.

What's the value of vulnerability to your bottom line? It's loyalty. Loyalty leads to sales. Every. Single. Time.

CHAPTER 30: PERSISTENCE

"the quality that allows someone to continue doing something or trying to do something even though it is difficult or opposed by other people"
Merriam-Webster[81]

Persistence. It may be the strongest drive. In many ways, it's the less sexy version of hope. Right? My mom always sings this song about an ant trying to move a rubber tree plant (High Hopes). Well, he may have hope, but he doesn't quit at the first sign of trouble. Part of the chorus is, "Oops, there goes another rubber tree plant." Meaning, this ant is trying to move a plant way too large even for him, and it's crashed to the ground. Again. So maybe hope and persistence are the same. Why is a person persistent? And can persistence be good? By the way, what does any of this have to do with social media?

Likely, persistence and hope are extrinsically tied together. Why else would you pursue a seemingly insurmountable obstacle?

Persistence Builds Endurance

Nothing is ever achieved that is great without sacrifice, naysayers, or pain. Think about great inventors and Olympic athletes. If science didn't persist, we'd still think that Earth was the center of the universe. If you look back at the people who inspire you, they almost always triumph over great odds. We love these types of stories -- the victory of the underdog. Did all of those people have a glimmer of hope?

Identify The Obstacles

Those of us who are perfectionists use perfection as an excuse not to start. We procrastinate by doing research or by optimizing our time. We often want our product to be amazing right out of the gate. I'm a hybrid. Yeah, I like things that I do to be done well, but I'm also a "something is better than nothing" kind of a person. So, I have a war within. The naysayers could be your family, friends, coworkers, boss. But, for writers, I think the naysayer is within. Instead of focusing on the obstacle, focus on the goal -- that's hope.

Commitment To Persistence

I'll use myself as an example, not for you to pull out your collective violins, but because it's kinder. So, this site/blog maybe gets 20 hits a day. And publishing once a week hasn't put a dent in that. So, I'll say to myself, "Who even cares if I keep publishing on Saturdays? Probably no one even expects it."

So, yeah, I didn't plan, and I'm booked up all weekend. Thursday at 6:30 a.m. is the only time I have to write. Firstly, if you set a goal, then you should continue. If not for your audience, but yourself. Secondly, writing (insert your challenge here) gets better with practice. Sure, maybe this one article isn't going to win me an award.

What are my real goals? Not all goals are tangible. If I look back at why I started this blog in the first place, it teaches and encourages. So, hits are not relevant to me.

Comments and tweets from people who continue because they felt inspired and empowered are my ROI. It's not about Google Analytics for me. So why am I up early? Because I said I would publish. And I'm going to. For you. For me. Because: Persistence. Because maybe what I said will help one person.

The Social Media Long Game

It took me long enough to get here, but I've said it frequently: social media is a long game. It is not instant. If you need to produce something with instant or semi-instant results, try knitting, baking, or carpentry. (Actually, quite a few creatives I know have those types of projects going on.) If you are pursuing social media to develop relationships that will turn into leads as part of your business development, keep going. If you feel stuck or like you're in a rut, hire a consultant to get you back on track. Take an online class. Join a meetup. There are plenty of resources available to you -- both free and paid -- that can help you continue. Giving up because "Twitter doesn't work" or "blogging didn't work" is frankly lame at best. You may need to work on your tactics just a tiny bit to increase your effectiveness. You wouldn't want to quit mining one inch from the gold vein, right?

What's your rubber tree plant?

For you, it might be spending time optimizing your Twitter lists. It could be attending more networking events. My rubber tree plant is publishing content every week. To overcome it, you need to identify the opposition, figure out how to persist, and do.

FINAL
THOUGHTS

You made it here, friend. You've read the whole book. You've scribbled in the margins and applied some of the lessons to your actions. You've tweeted and commented and published articles.

What happens now? What do you do next?

The next step, if you haven't done it yet, is reflection. Bonus points for answering these questions in a journal. The answers determine your voice, brand guidelines, and even your business model.

- How do I want my business to be seen online?
- Do I put people first in my business? Customers? Employees?
- What are the topics I care most about?
- How can I make time to publish regularly?

- Do I have someone on staff who can help with social? Can they be promoted?
- Am I looking for a fast buck or am I determined to make an impact?
- How do my decisions affect customer perception?
- Will I be proud of my online presence in ten years?

If you'd like help reaching some of these answers, feel free to reach out to me at bridgetwillard.com or find a business coach or accountability partner. Sometimes it feels like we are alone, but I promise you, we aren't. You aren't. You started your business for a reason.

You got this.

BIBLIOGRAPHY

Anacan, R. (n.d.). *Would You Wear a 'Snuggie' on a First Date?* MultifamilyInsiders.com. Retrieved Oct 7, 2020, from https://www.multifamilyinsiders.com/multifamily-blogs/how-would-you-dress-for-a-first-date

Aungst, P. (n.d.). *The Secret Power of Secret Facebook Groups.* PamAnnMarketing.com. Retrieved Oct 7, 2020, from https://pamannmarketing.com/the-secret-power-of-secret-facebook-groups/

Baer, D. (n.d.). *Why Productive Teams Have 3 Kinds of Diversity.* FastCompany.com. Retrieved Oct 7, 2020, from https://www.fastcompany.com/3015112/why-productive-teams-have-3-kinds-of-diversity

Brown, B. (n.d.). *The Power of Vulnerability.* TED. Re-

trieved Oct 7, 2020, from https://www.ted.com/talks/
brene_brown_the_power_of_vulnerability/transcript

Clark, B. (n.d.). *15 Grammar Goofs That Make You Look
Silly [Infographic]*. CopyBlogger.com. Retrieved Oct 7,
2020, from https://copyblogger.com/grammar-goofs/

Cuddy, A. (n.d.). *our body language shapes who
you are*. TED.com. Retrieved Oct 7, 2020,
from https://www.ted.com/talks/amy_cuddy_your_
body_language_may_shape_who_you_are?language=en

Electronic Frontier Foundation. (n.d.). *Intellectual Prop-
erty*. Eff.org. https://www.eff.org/issues/bloggers/legal/
liability/IP

Fout, A. (n.d.). *Death of a Perfectionist*. Blue Steele Solutions. Retrieved Oct 7, 2020, from https://bluesteeleso-
lutions.com/death-of-a-perfectionst/

The Free Dictionary. (n.d.). *Vulnerability*. The Free Dictionary. Retrieved Oct 7, 2020, from https://www.the-

freedictionary.com/vulnerability

Internet Live Stats. (n.d.). *Twitter Usage Statistics*. Internet Live Stats. Retrieved Oct 7, 2020, from https://www.internetlivestats.com/twitter-statistics/

Isopo, R. (n.d.). *One Thing That All Students Need to Be Taught: Manners*. PressReader.com. Retrieved Oct 7, 2020, from https://www.pressreader.com/canada/montreal-gazette/20130621/281848641171809

Johnson, S. (n.d.). *Where Good Ideas Come From*. TED.com. Retrieved 7, Oct, from https://www.ted.com/talks/steven_johnson_where_good_ideas_come_from

Klocek, S. (n.d.). *Better together; the practice of successful creative collaboration*. Stefanklocek.com. Retrieved Oct 7, 2020, from http://www.stefanklocek.com/better-together-the-practice-of-successful-creative-collaboration/

Kramer, B., & Rubin, T. (n.d.). *Substance: Connecting with*

Your Customer with Ted Rubin, CMO of Brand Innovators. YouTube.com. Retrieved 7, Oct, from https://youtu.be/ DCZeOyBwuys

Lapowsky, I. (n.d.). *Gary Vaynerchuk: How to Tell Your Story on Social Media.* Inc.com. Retrieved Oct 7, 2020, from https://www.inc.com/issie-lapowsky/gary-vayner-chuk-how-to-get-heard-on-social-media.html

Maxwell, J. C. (2010). *Everyone Communicates, Few Connect.* (1st ed.). Thomas Nelson.

Merriam-Webster. (n.d.). *Authentic.* Merriam-Webster.com. Retrieved Oct 7, 2020, from https://www.merriam-webster.com/dictionary/authentic

Merriam-Webster. (n.d.). *Encouragement.* Merriam-Webster. Retrieved Oct 7, 2020, from https://www.merriam-webster.com/dictionary/encouragement

Merriam-Webster. (n.d.). *Honor.* Merriam-Webster.com. Retrieved October 7, 2020, from https://www.merriam-webster.com/dictionary/honor.

Merriam-Webster. (n.d.). *Influence*. Merriam-Webster.com. Retrieved Oct 7, 2020, from https://www.merriam-webster.com/dictionary/influence

Merriam-Webster. (n.d.). *Persistence*. Merriam-Webster.com Dictionary. Retrieved Oct 7, 2020, from https://www.merriam-webster.com/dictionary/persistence

Merriam-Webster. (n.d.). *Responsibility*. Merriam-Webster.com. Retrieved Oct 7, 2020, from https://www.merriam-webster.com/dictionary/responsibility

On Point with Tom Ashbrook. (n.d.). *How We're Talking, Like, Today*. WUBR.org. Retrieved Oct 7, 20, from https://www.wbur.org/onpoint/2014/01/23/vocal-fry-verbal-tics-language

Rusine, R. (n.d.). *Keys to Being Social Honor*. Business 2 Community. https://www.business2community.com/content-marketing/keys-social-honor-0731933

Simmons, M. (n.d.). *To Create a Real Connection Show Vulnerability*. Harvard Business Review. Retrieved Oct 7, 2020, from https://hbr.org/2014/05/to-create-a-real-connection-show-vulnerability

Sinek, S. (n.d.). *Why Good Leaders Make You Feel Safe*. TEDEd. Retrieved Oct 7, 2020, from https://ed.ted.com/lessons/why-good-leaders-make-you-feel-safe-simon-sinek

Sivers, D. (n.d.). *Obvious to you. Amazing to others*. You-Tube.com. Retrieved Oct 7, 2020, from https://youtu.be/xcmI5SSQLmE

Stephen, C. (n.d.). *Five Hidden Benefits of Listening*. Business 2 Community. Retrieved Oct 7, 2020, from https://www.business2community.com/social-media/five-hidden-benefits-listening-01169676

Stephen, C. (n.d.). *Social Media New Ways to Fail*. YourSocialMediaWorks.com. Retrieved Oct 7, 2020, from http://yoursocialmediaworks.com/social-media-new-ways-to-fail

Stratten, S. (n.d.). *Mannequin Networking*. UnMarketing.com. https://unmarketing.com/2010/02/18/mannequin-networking/

Vaynerchuk, G. (n.d.). *How To Produce Content for Vine*. GaryVaynerchuk.com. Retrieved Oct 7, 2020, from https://www.garyvaynerchuk.com/infographic-getting-weird-on-vine/

Vaynerchuk, G. (n.d.). *Why You Really Need to Subscribe to My Channel*. YouTube.com. Retrieved Oct 7, 2020, from https://youtu.be/amyoaSLwwVU

Victore, J. (n.d.). *Op-Ed: Confidence vs Shyness*. 99u.com. Retrieved Oct 7, 2020, from https://99u.adobe.com/articles/7164/op-ed-confidence-vs-shyness

Vital, A. (n.d.). *Why We Live – Counting The People Your Life Impacts [Infographic]*. Adioma.com. Retrieved Oct

7, 2020, from https://blog.adioma.com/counting-the-people-you-impact-infographic/

Wallis, L. (n.d.). *Is 25 The New Cut Off Point for Adulthood.* BBC News. Retrieved Oct 7, 2020, from https://www.bbc.com/news/magazine-24173194

Wikipedia. (n.d.). *Influencer Marketing.* Wikipedia. Retrieved Oct 7, 2020, from https://en.wikipedia.org/wiki/Influencer_marketing

Willard, B. (n.d.). *Why I Don't Use Twitter's Retweet Button.* BridgetWillard.com. Retrieved Oct 7, 2020, from https://bridgetwillard.com/why-i-dont-use-twitters-retweet-button/

---

[1] (Merriam-Webster.com Dictionary, n.d.)
[2] (Rusine, n.d.) Original Blog Post for Ruby Rusine is now a 404 error.

[3] Spoken at a Meetup. Referenced in this article. (Rusine, n.d.)

[4] (Electronic Frontier Foundation, n.d.)

[5] Private Video http://youtu.be/OXtc-jBSg_U

[6] https://twitter.com/rigginsconst

[7] https://twitter.com/search?q=%23EngageFriday&src=typed_query&f=live

[8] https://twitter.com/search?q=%23FF&src=typed_query&f=live

[9] (Original blog post by Amy Donohue no longer exists.)

[10] (Stephen, n.d.)

[11] http://www.allencbuchanan.com/

[12] http://www.rigginsconst.com/

[13] https://twitter.com/zenproverbs/status/447223067946008576

[14] https://www.afcpromos.com/

[15] https://www.goodreads.com/quotes/1629-it-is-the-mark-of-an-educated-mind-to-be

[16] https://twitter.com/search?q=%23FF&src=typed_query

[17] (Willard, n.d.)

[18] https://www.garyvaynerchuk.com/

[19] (Vaynerchuk, n.d.)

[20] https://www.snapchat.com/add/garyvee

[21] (Lapowsky, n.d.)

[22] https://twitter.com/Carol_Stephen

[23] https://twitter.com/kendra_hubbard

[24] https://twitter.com/search?q=%23solarchat&src=typed_query&f=live

[25] (Merriam-Webster, n.d.)

[26] https://youtu.be/cfwwHa-7Ux8

[27] (Anacan, n.d.)

[28] (Stratten, n.d.)

[29] (On Point with Tom Ashbrook, n.d.)

[30] https://twitter.com/unmarketing/status/427503756717342720

[31] (Original Tweet has been deleted.)

[32] (Merriam-Webster, n.d.)

[33] https://www.brainyquote.com/quotes/steve_jobs_416881

[34] (Aungst, n.d.)

[35] (Victore, n.d.)

[36] (Cuddy, n.d.)

[37] (Cuddy, n.d.)

[38] https://www.brainyquote.com/quotes/henry_wadsworth_longfello_138607

[39] https://fabamy.wordpress.com/2012/07/10/whats-the-difference-between-facebook-and-twitter/

[40] https://twitter.com/ChefIvanFlowers

[41] (Sivers, n.d.)

[42] https://tesswittler.com/stuff/lp-52-content-ideas/

[43] https://www.goodreads.com/quotes/294967-enthusiasm-is-one-of-the-most-powerful-engines-of-success

[44] (Vaynerchuk, n.d.)

[45] (Vaynerchuk, n.d.)

[46] https://www.brainyquote.com/quotes/oscar_wilde_101035

[47] Here is my tutorial: https://youtu.be/k1JWRkTbrLY

[48] https://www.powerquotations.com/quote/humor-is-a-spontaneous-wonderful

[49] (Clark, n.d.)

[50] (Maxwell, 2010, Not sure of the page number.)

[51] Article is a 404 now https://thecontractorstoolbox.com

[52] This blog post is a 404 now. https://aaronhockley.com

[53] Original Post is a 404. (Stratten, n.d.)

[54] https://www.brainyquote.com/quotes/confucius_136805

[55] (Isopo, n.d.)

[56] (Kramer & Rubin, n.d.)

[57] (Wallis, n.d.)

[58] https://twitter.com/search?q=%23BufferChat&src=typed_query

[59] http://twitter.com/buffer/status/580766344989306881

[60] (Internet Live Stats, n.d.)

[61] (Stephen, n.d.)

[62] (Baer, n.d.)

[63] (Klocek, n.d.)

[64] (Johnson, n.d.)

[65] danielnorris.com (Quote could no longer be found.)

[66] (Merriam-Webster, n.d.)

[67] (Vital, n.d.)

[68] (Wikipedia, n.d.)

[69] (Merriam-Webster, n.d.)

[70] (Brown, n.d.)

[71] (The Free Dictionary, n.d.)

[72] https://twitter.com/carinarrigo

[73] (Brown, n.d.)

[74] https://www.amazon.com/Come-Away-Bridget-Willard/dp/B000CA7FSS

[75] He produced my album "Come Away" 2003 chrisfalson.com/

[76] (Simmons, n.d.)

[77] (Simmons, n.d.)

[78] (Sinek, n.d.)

[79] I heard her say this in person. https://twitter.com/tamiheaton

[80] (Fout, n.d.)

[81] (Merriam-Webster, n.d.)

ACKNOWLEDGE-MENT

Thank you, Sarah Phillips, for pushing me way beyond what I believed I was capable with the editing of this book.

Cover design by Rhonda Negard of FatDogCreatives.com.

ABOUT THE AUTHOR

Bridget Willard

Bridget Willard is a marketing consultant who brings her teaching and accounting background together to help small businesses. She began her marketing career in construction, then worked in franchise development, nonprofits, and tech. She is especially known for her brand building for Riggins Construction, GiveWP, and the Make WordPress Marketing Team.

Bridget co-hosts The Smart Marketing Show with Jason Tucker -- a podcast and live YouTube show on the WPwatercooler network.

When she's not writing about marketing or social media, she is spending time with her friends, changing her hair style, learning languages on Duolingo, or walking outside.

Say hi to her on Twitter at @youtoocanbeguru and check out her site at bridgetwillard.com.